GOVERNING
OUR FIFTY STATES
AND
THEIR COMMUNITIES

**FOUNDATIONS OF AMERICAN GOVERNMENT
AND POLITICAL SCIENCE**

Joseph P. Harris, Consulting Editor

Revisions and additions have been made to keep this series up to date and to enlarge its scope, but its purpose remains the same as it was on first publication: To provide a group of relatively short treatises dealing with major aspects of government in modern society. Each volume introduces the reader to a major field of political science through a discussion of important issues, problems, processes, and forces and includes at the same time an account of American political institutions. The author of each work is a distinguished scholar who specializes in and teaches the subjects covered. Together the volumes are well adapted to serving the needs of introductory courses in American government and political science.

ANDREW HACKER   The Study of Politics: The Western Tradition and American Origins

C. HERMAN PRITCHETT   The American Constitutional System, 3d ed.

HUGH A. BONE and AUSTIN RANNEY   Politics and Voters, 3d ed.

ROWLAND EGGER   The President of the United States, 2d ed.

JOSEPH P. HARRIS   Congress and the Legislative Process, 2d ed.

JOHN J. CORSON and JOSEPH P. HARRIS   Public Administration in Modern Society

CHARLES O. LERCHE, JR.   America in World Affairs, 2d ed.

CHARLES R. ADRIAN   Governing Our Fifty States and Their Communities, 3d ed.

H. FRANK WAY, JR.   Liberty in the Balance: Current Issues in Civil Liberties, 3d ed.

GOVERNING
OUR FIFTY STATES
AND
THEIR COMMUNITIES

THIRD EDITION

CHARLES R. ADRIAN
PROFESSOR OF POLITICAL SCIENCE
UNIVERSITY OF CALIFORNIA, RIVERSIDE

McGRAW-HILL BOOK COMPANY
New York   San Francisco   St. Louis   Düsseldorf   Johannesburg
Kuala Lumpur   London   Mexico   Montreal   New Delhi   Panama
Rio de Janeiro   Singapore   Sydney   Toronto

This book was set in Helvetica by Rocappi, Inc., and printed on permanent paper and bound by George Banta Company. The designer was Janet Bollow. The editors were Robert P. Rainier and Michael A. Ungersma. Charles A. Goehring supervised production.

GOVERNING
OUR FIFTY STATES
AND
THEIR COMMUNITIES

Library of Congress catalog card number: 78-174608

1234567890 BABA 798765432

PREFACE

This third edition incorporates, wherever possible, the latest research and policy developments. In particular, attention has been given to recent information concerning legislative behavior, reapportionment, and community decision making. While the treatment has been brought up to date, the basic approach of the first edition still holds.

American government can be understood as a system of institutions for social control only if it is examined at all three levels—national, state, and local. This brief study does not attempt to cover the whole of the vast area of governmental responsibilities, but addresses itself to the functioning of the two subsystems and seeks to relate them and their activities to those of the third, the federal. State legislatures resemble Congress in many ways, yet there are distinctions. The governorship imitates the Presidency to a degree, but is different in kind, too. State courts share many—but by no means all—characteristics with federal courts. Bureaucracies have more in common than they have to distinguish one from another, but some of the differences are of considerable significance. In noting the similarities and distinctions, stress has been placed not upon mechanical details, encyclopedic description, or superficial comparisons, but rather upon the unique characteristics of state and local governments in the total decision-making process.

The obvious brevity of the work perhaps makes it unnecessary to apologize for omissions and condensations of material that might well have had greater development. Responsibility for the selection of certain subjects for emphasis, however, and any errors of fact rest entirely with me.

CHARLES R. ADRIAN

CONTENTS

1 THE LEGAL SETTING

State and local governments are an integral part of the complex American political system. They must be studied with a constant awareness of or reference to the total setting. There is much overlap in institutions and processes between national and state and local governments. The emphasis in this brief work will therefore be on the differences rather than the similarities. The latter are covered in detail elsewhere, including the companion volumes in this series.

COOPERATIVE FEDERALISM
The federal, state, and local governments have all expanded their activities during the history of the nation, but particularly in the past two generations. The federal government, especially since the Great

Depression which began in the fall of 1929, has authorized a multitude of regulatory and service activities that once existed only in rudimentary form, if at all. In addition, Congress with its great financial resources has sought to assist state and local governments by providing a growing number of grants-in-aid. Over the years, the distinctions between federal and nonfederal activities, which were once attempted by judges, editors, and others and which were enforced to a degree by the courts, have been disappearing. The practice of the nineteenth century was to leave most responsibilities to individuals and corporations. Government's small share was divided up, in the model if not always in practice, among three levels of government, each responsible for its specific tasks. After the Great Depression, the standard practice has been not that of *dividing* up power, but rather of allowing decisions about many of the activities of our society to be *shared* by all three levels of government (cooperative federalism), as well as sometimes with private individuals, corporate management, and private voluntary organizations, including such important groups as labor unions and community chest agencies.

The concepts of dual federalism and state sovereignty, which tended to see the various levels of government held separate in watertight compartments, have been rendered obsolete by post-Depression developments. This has caused some citizens to conclude that state and local governments are no longer important. In fact, however, their significance has been increasing in the new task of these governments as functional parts of a system of federalism.

The states and their communities will continue into the future as partners with the federal government in an informal system of cooperative federalism. Of course, with federal military expenditures making up a large part of the economy, with federal grants expanding into new areas at each session of Congress, and with the superior fiscal power of the federal government, it would be unrealistic to suggest that they will in the future increase in importance relative to the federal government. The significant thing is that they *are* important and will continue to be important.

The emphasis at the state and local levels is upon domestic rather than foreign policy and, within that context, upon the refinement of existing policies. Although decision making about domestic policies, under the existing pattern of cooperative federalism, is a joint undertaking involving all levels of government, policy innovation is most likely to come through the institutions of the federal government. In general, interests prefer to make their contacts there, and for a number of reasons:

1. As a Presidential study commission has pointed out, "many State constitutions restrict the scope, effectiveness, and adaptability of state and local action. These self-imposed constitutional limitations make it difficult for many states to perform all of the services citizens require, and consequently have frequently been the underlying cause of state and municipal pleas for Federal assistance."[1]

2. Congress is generally more oriented toward urban problems than are state legislatures, which until recently were dominated by small-town representatives inexperienced with these problems and with viewpoints not sympathetic toward the expansion of governmental activities.

3. The federal tax structure is such that the marginal cost of a new program is less at that level than it is at state and local levels, where there is greater fiscal rigidity.

4. A victory at the federal level is likely to mean that a new or expanded program will be applied throughout the nation—a more efficient approach to action than are time- and effort-consuming separate appeals to 50 states or hundreds of local governments. The states and localities, furthermore, cannot easily change policies if they involve federal grants-in-aid, lest they risk jeopardizing revenues. The federal government, on the other hand, can make changes quite easily. Its leaders must act within considerations of political expediency—too much pressure on the states will be politically unpopular and congressmen quickly become aware of really serious opposition—but federal decision makers have far more potential flexibility than do their state and local colleagues.

THE BALANCE OF FEDERALISM

For a great many years, the question of the balance of federalism in America has been debated. The controversy involves both the matter of the actual trends in the balance and that of the desirability or undesirability of various possible trends. Some writers profess to see a

[1] Commission on Intergovernmental Relations (the Kestnbaum Commission), *A Report to the President,* 1955, p. 37.

constantly declining level of importance of the states and their subdivisions; others see some changes, but with the lesser units retaining their vitality and importance. There are those who bemoan the supposed decline of the states and their subdivisions, and others who would gladly see the end of any independence of the states as a supposedly necessary prelude to more effective American government with a fully responsible central authority. It is fortunate that some empirical evidence exists concerning the current relationship of the federal government to the states and their subdivisions.

SOME FINANCIAL MEASURES   Federal domestic program expenditures during the period of 1949 to 1962 show an increase of 133 percent. The relative burden of this upon the individual and the economy has been minimized by the rapid expansion of the nation's economy. Gross national product—GNP—or the total annual addition to the value of the nation's goods and services without allowances for taxes or depreciation, went from 257 billion dollars in 1949 to 443 billion dollars in 1957, and 971 billion dollars in 1970. Expanding budgets have not represented substantial federal government cuts into income usually allotted by society for other purposes. In the past generation, federal domestic programs have consumed only about 2 percent of our annual GNP.

THE TREND IN STATE AND LOCAL EXPENDITURES   The fact that federal domestic expenditures have been increasing does not, in itself, give any clue to the trend in the balance of federalism. Federal spending has been moving boldly upward, but the same trend is to be found on the state and local levels. Between 1948 and 1962, while federal domestic expenditures were increasing by 133 percent on a per capita, constant-dollar basis, state and local expenditures increased by 95 percent. The robust American economy of the postwar years, with GNP expanding faster than the population, has absorbed most of this increase, as it has that on the federal level.

GRANTS-IN-AID AND THE BALANCE OF FEDERALISM   One more vital area remains to be examined before tentative conclusions can be drawn concerning the postwar trend in national-state-local relations. This is relative to the much-discussed matter of the effect of grants-in-aid upon the balance of federalism.

The data indicate that federal grants-in-aid have increased considerably in the postwar years. Between fiscal 1948 and 1962, they expanded by 355 percent in per capita, constant-dollar terms. They increased at a much higher rate than did federal domestic expenditures, which advanced by 133 percent during the same period. Federal grants represented a higher percentage of the total federal government budget as compared with the preceding year in most years, between 1952 and 1962. The grants also increased as a percentage of GNP in most calendar years between 1951 and 1971. Factors other than these, however, are probably more important in determining the significance of the use of grants upon the balance of federalism. For one thing, grants have become an exceptionally *inflexible* portion of the federal government budget. To date, this inflexibility appears not to have had serious consequences, but the fact that grants, in a typical year, make up nearly 40 percent of the federal domestic budget would indicate that this phenomenon may eventually have important consequences for democracy and for the national-state-local balance.

The increased number of federal grants In 1970, around 80 different grants-in-aid were offered by the federal government to state and local governments. (The total number depended upon the way in which separate programs were defined.) Probably the most important trend in the use of grants-in-aid is toward a proliferation of their number. The bulk of increased grant expenditures has come in the well-established fields of agriculture, education, highways, public welfare, and housing. The agricultural program increases have been substantial, but they have come largely through expansions in long-existing programs, especially through the 1955 amendments to the Hatch Act, which, beginning in 1887, has provided the basic support for agricultural experiment stations, and through the extensive rewriting in 1953 of the Smith-Lever Act of 1914 providing for the cooperative agricultural extension program.[2]

[2] Rebecca L. Notz, *Federal Grants-in-aid to States,* Council of State Governments, Chicago, 1956, lists all federal grants to 1956; W. Brooke Graves, *American Intergovernmental Relations,* Charles Scribner's Sons, New York, 1964, Appendix A, lists them through 1962. Since then, see the publications of the Advisory Commission on Intergovernmental Relations.

Housing grants date from 1937, but they were expanded by the Housing Acts of 1949 and 1954. In highways, grants have been a familiar part of the picture since 1916, but the Federal-Aid Highway Act of 1956 provided for a greatly expanded program in the coming years. Pleas for and against the federal government's "entering" the field of aid to education have tended to obscure the fact that at least 25 federal grant programs were already in existence in 1957 in the field of education. The Federal Aid-to-Education Act of 1965 only reinforced a long trend. Public-welfare grants have been broadened in scope by frequent new legislation in the years since 1933.

Although these expanding older programs are themselves important, more significant implications for the future may perhaps be seen in the fact that almost every postwar session of Congress has added to the number of grants.

Grants as a portion of state-local expenditures Despite the tendency toward an increase in their number, grants have not become a significantly more important portion of total state and local expenditures in postwar years. The prevailing practice has been to spread the grants across the domestic-program panorama in a thin glaze.

Two other tendencies were pointed out by the Eisenhower-appointed Kestnbaum Commission on Intergovernmental Relations. That group noted a postwar tendency for grants "to recognize varying state fiscal capacity," that is, to make the size of the grant vary inversely with the state's ability to pay. This is in contrast to the almost universal prewar practice of distributing funds according to the amount of service needed and, with equalization as a justifying argument, may offer a basis for additional future grants in many areas. The commission also noted that nearly all grants have some strings attached to them, many of them highly important in their potential effect upon policy. Furthermore, "the conditions attached to grants have not remained mere verbal expressions of national intent; national agencies have generally had funds and staff to make them effective."

The impact of federal grants Many a writer has led his readers through a veritable chamber of horrors in discussing the dangers to be found in expanded federal influence upon domestic programs. Actually, however, the grants voted in postwar years may have *aided* decentralization of decision making and hence contributed to the viability of the federal system. The fact is that the actual impact of federal grants upon policy is not known. In the absence of further study, the implications of the postwar rash of grant programs cannot be confidently discussed. The more important question of the 1970s is that of what would be the effect of block grants provided by the federal government to states for distribution as they see fit—with no strings attached. Such grants were first proposed in the early 1960s by the Kennedy administration and were endorsed in 1971 by President Nixon, but their desirability and effect upon the federal system remained controversial.

FEDERAL GOVERNMENT RELATIONS WITH STATE AND COMMUNITY

The federal government has a great many contacts with the states and their subdivisions in the administration of governmental programs outside the fiscal area. Collectively, these contacts reflect the present trend toward the cooperation of administrative officers at all levels of government in seeking to provide socially wanted services despite the arbitrariness of political boundaries and the inappropriate distribution of tax resources among the various units of government.

Whenever the states or any of their subdivisions are involved in activities over which the federal government has final jurisdiction, they must conform to federal regulations. Similarly, they must agree to the strings that are often attached whenever a grant-in-aid is accepted.

The list of federal supervisory controls is almost endless. However, before reaching the easy conclusion that the federal government makes all of the rules in modern American society, it should be pointed out that the areas of federal control are relatively few compared to the total number possible and that it is not politically expedient for Congress or federal administrators to impose or enforce many effective policy controls upon the states or their subdivisions. Furthermore, administrators at all levels often see themselves as being involved in a cooperative venture to apply professional standards and do not feel coerced. Despite the impression that is often created, federal administrators usually try to be reasonable in administering the law and seek to work out problems jointly rather than by fiat. Still, in the event of an unresolved difference between a federal agency and the state or local government with which it is dealing, the federal requirements must be met if the state or local government wishes to qualify for federal aid. Furthermore, in all areas of activity, including those not involving intergovernmental payments, the courts will normally support federal law ("the supreme law of the land") in cases of conflict with the laws of other levels of government.

THE LEGAL BASIS OF LOCAL GOVERNMENTS

The legal position of a local unit of government has been succinctly described by the United States Supreme Court as that of "a political subdivision of the state, created as a convenient agency for the exercise of such of the governmental powers of the state as may be intrusted to it." All local governments, unless they enjoy special status in state constitutions, are simply creatures of the state. They can perform only those functions assigned to them, and by long tradition the state courts tend to interpret narrowly their powers.

Cities, villages, and sometimes counties, are, in some states, given the power to frame, adopt, and amend their own charters, that is, to enjoy the right of local "home rule." But even in these cases, the usual rule is that this freedom extends only to the structure of government—the legislature still decides the powers to be exercised by local units. In a few states, however, these units are given powers over matters of "local concern" and this term is defined by the courts rather than the legislature. These examples are the exception, however. Most local governments are, legally, children of the state.

CONSTITUTIONS: THE RULE BOOKS OF THE POLITICAL GAME

The constitution is the fundamental law of each state. Its principal purposes are (1) to describe the basic structure of government and (2) to allocate political power. This allocation must be made among levels of government, among branches of government, and between government and the individual. In each constitution, the state government and various types of local governments are established with a statement of their general powers and relationships to one another. Every state government is established with the familiar distribution of authority according to the principle of the separation of powers among the executive, legislative, and judicial branches. And, as with the United States Constitution, some powers are given to government, while others, known as civil rights, are withheld from it to prevent government from encroaching on the rights of individuals. In addition, state constitutions contain many restrictions on the taxing, procedural, and substantive powers of state and local government.

Constitutions are political documents. The very fact that they help determine the rules of politics in itself makes them the object of manipulation by the various interests that make up society. Their content is constantly a matter of concern to groups and individuals, and since constitutions are more difficult to change than statute laws, groups seek to protect their special interests by incorporating them, whenever possible, into the fundamental law of the state.

AMENDING STATE CONSTITUTIONS A state constitution can be amended in a great variety of ways:

1. Like the United States Constitution, it can be changed through executive, legislative, and judicial interpretation. This is, in fact, probably the most important means of changing it. For example, a governor may himself interpret a vague provision concerning his powers; legislative leaders often give on-the-spot interpretations of the constitution during debates; courts apply the constitution routinely through judicial review.

2. A constitutional convention may recommend changes to be ratified through the regular amending process of the existing constitution. It may also submit an entirely new or largely rewritten document for ratification. Many state constitutions have provisions allowing for a referendum on the question of calling a state constitutional convention. In others, the courts have held that the legislature may submit the question to the voters at its discretion. In some states, the question is required to be submitted periodically. Sometimes a "commission," which is a miniature convention, may be appointed by the legislature, the governor, or jointly by both in order to submit proposals.

3. Thirteen states allow voters to propose constitutional amendments through use of the *initiative*. Under this plan, action is required by a convention or by the legislature. A petition is circulated stating the proposal. If enough signatures are obtained to satisfy the law, the proposal is placed directly upon the ballot at the next election.

The initiated constitutional amendment is not common, but the procedure is important because it marks a drastic departure from the more common rules. It may, for example, permit the submission to the voters of proposals that would not be approved by a conservative legislature.

4. By far the most common means of proposing amendments to state constitutions is through submission by the legislature. Every state except New Hampshire authorizes this method. It usually involves a resolution by the legislature, commonly requiring two-thirds or three-fifths of the membership to vote in favor. This requirement, of course, makes passage difficult. A few states allow an amendment to be submitted by the vote of a simple majority in each house; but nine states require a majority vote in two successive sessions, and this is often a major obstacle to change. In states with biennial sessions, it may delay amendment for as long as four years.

RATIFICATION OF AMENDMENTS Typically, a proposed amendment is adopted by a simple majority of those voting on the question. This is the case in about 35 states. Others require an extraordinary majority: of those voting in the election (failure to vote on the constitutional question is thus an automatic "no" vote), for example. Illinois, Rhode Island, and Tennessee require approval by some figure greater than 50 percent plus one vote. In Delaware, the legislature can propose an amendment at one session and can adopt it by approving it again at a succeeding session. South Carolina and Mississippi, states with strong elite traditions, permit the legislature to make the final decision whether or not an amendment is to go into effect, even in cases where the popular vote has been in its favor.

POLITICS AND CONSTITUTIONAL VERBIAGE The United States Constitution is a brief document, and so were the early constitutions of the states. In 1800, the longest state constitution, that of Massachusetts, contained only about 12,000 words. In the 1970s, the longest constitution was that of Louisiana with more than 200,000 words. Some other states were not far behind. The Louisiana constitution of 1921 had more than 300 amendments in its first 35 years of existence. In contrast, the Tennessee constitution went unamended between 1870 and 1953, a period of 83 years.

There are many reasons for the expanding length of state constitutions. The fact that American legislatures, especially in the years since the Civil War, have not been fully trusted by the people has encouraged the writing of many rules restricting legislative powers. Constitutional provisions have been devised to control the legislature or to prevent it from acting in certain areas. In recent decades, this long-standing public attitude has, however, tended to come into conflict with the general desire for expanded governmental functions. The federal government was able to launch the scores of new programs of government since the 1930s without amending the United States Constitution, but a similar feat was not possible in most states where narrow judicial construction and specific restrictions of governmental powers required changes in the fundamental law before new programs could be established. Thus, constitutions grew in length initially in order to limit governmental power and later grew even more in order to ease existing restrictions.

Secondly, many state constitutions are relatively easy to amend, at least as compared with the federal constitution. (On the other hand, a few, such as those of Illinois and Tennessee, are very difficult to amend.) It is thus usually easier at the state level than at the federal to appeal from an unpopular judicial interpretation or legislative action by amending the fundamental law.

CONSTITUTION AND GROUP INTERESTS   Lastly, interest groups strongly desire to write their most favored policies into the constitution itself. Since a constitution is a set of rules about rule making, it should logically contain only enabling and prohibiting authority, in addition to a description of governmental structure. Upon this base, statute law (i.e., law formally enacted by a legislative body) would be built. In practice, however, groups within society learned during the nineteenth century that there was nothing except custom to prevent the inclusion of statute law in the constitutions themselves. With this understood, they began using constitutions for their own ends. Since these bodies of law are normally more difficult to amend than are statutes, they gave added protection to the major interests of groups. Furthermore, the fact that any constitutional provision enjoys a special aura of sanctity makes it more difficult for another group to mount a counterattack than would be the case if the provision were mere statute law.

It should not be assumed that an interest group, in putting one of its favorite pieces of legislation into the constitution, is seeking to achieve its goals by devious and deceptive means. In many cases, the group membership believes strongly in the particular piece of legislation and sincerely regards it as having a proper place in the fundamental law.

A great many interests have contributed to the length and complexity of constitutions. The general distrust of the legislature encouraged conventions from the 1850s onward to spell out state and local government organization in detail. Some of these provisions are now thought by many persons to be outmoded, but they cannot be changed by legislative action alone. Distrust also caused severe limitations to be placed, in many states, upon the power to tax and to incur debt. These provisions were reasonable in a day of corrupt legislatures and of simple government operations. Today, with many demands for increasing services, they become obstacles to public policy making.

Writing statute law into the constitution tends to increase its rigidity. The result is that sometimes an unrepresentative and outmoded law remains in force because the unusual efforts needed to change it cannot be made. On the other hand, where legislatures are unrepresentative, constitutional amendment may be the only, or at least the best, device for overcoming their refusal to act on legislation that has popular support.

THE DECLINE OF CONSTITUTION WRITING Before the second decade of the present century, rewriting state constitutions was part of the American way of life. From time to time, as population patterns changed within states, economic elites and social organization changed, or political values evolved, a tendency to write new state constitutions resulted. More than two hundred state constitutional conventions have met.

Yet, after World War I, the old pattern of periodic rewriting of the fundamental law came to an end. Between 1920 and 1960, excluding

Alaska and Hawaii, only seven constitutions were adopted. Why this change? The answer is probably to be found principally in the rapid urbanization of the nation after that time and in the clustering of urban populations around a relatively few metropolitan areas. With this trend came an increasing social heterogeneity and declining consensus of values among citizens. Residents of rural areas, villages, and small cities, who were overrepresented as a result, recognized that a complete reappraisal of state government by a constitutional convention selected on the basis of population could result in a considerable loss of their influence in state government. In order to retain the disproportionate power they possessed through the accident of shifting populations, persons in these areas opposed constitutional revision. It is also likely that, as statute law has accumulated in the state constitutions through time, a larger and larger number of groups came to possess a vested interest in retaining the existing document and in not risking the unknown in a convention. Urban conservatives, furthermore, sometimes found it to their advantage to leave state government in the hands of small-towners whose preference for minimal governmental activities is in accord with their own desires.

Court-imposed reapportionment of state legislatures (see Chapter 4) changed the practice of avoiding the holding of state constitutional conventions. Urban- and suburban-dominated legislatures are now more willing to have such conventions meet and we may thus be returning to practices more in the American tradition. Rhode Island, in 1964, was the first state to hold a convention after the courts assumed jurisdiction in the matter of apportionment. Since then, at least one state has held a constitutional convention each year. No dramatic changes have taken place in public policies since the adoption of the "one man, one vote" rule.

REVIEW QUESTIONS

1. What are some of the reasons for the development of "cooperative federalism"?

2. How have federal grant-in-aid programs affected state and local powers of government?

3. Are federal grants-in-aid actually increasing in number and importance? Why or why not?

4. Give some examples of the way in which federal government activities affect state and local governments. Note whether or not federal money payments are involved in each of your examples.

5. What functions are served by state constitutions?

6. Describe the methods of amending state constitutions as compared with the federal constitution.

7. How is the constitution of your state amended?

8. Explain why most state constitutions are longer than the federal constitution.

9. What portions of your state constitution reflect small-town and suburban domination of past constitutional conventions?

2 STATE AND LOCAL FUNCTIONS AND FINANCE

The activities of state and local governments, like those at the national level, deal with the political questions of "who gets what, when, how." They are concerned with the "authoritative allocation of values"—of goods, services, privileges, and rules of the game, and can generally be classified into three categories: those that provide amenities to make life easier and more pleasant for the citizen (such as street lighting, garbage removal, or modern highways); social services (such as those related to public health, education, and welfare); and economic regulation and public safety (such as the supervision of the insurance business and the detention of criminals). In trying to detail the activities that fit these categories, we might find the task easier if we ask what state and local governments do *not* do. They are not involved directly in foreign policy or in foreign economic or military aid. They are not responsible for national defense, though they do bear a good share of the residual costs of World War I, World War II, and the Korean and Vietnamese conflicts, for they offer a variety of programs for veterans.

State and local governments not only provide the machinery for the settlement of most legal cases involving civil and criminal law, for the keeping of vital statistics, land ownership and other records, and for virtually all sanitation and fire protection services, but they are also basically responsible for education, streets and highways, and police protection. In addition, they pay for more than one-half of the cost of public expenditures in the areas of public health, public hospitals, parks, recreation, and public welfare.

We see at once some of the reasons why the public thinks of Washington when it thinks of "government" and why state and local governments are sometimes mistakenly thought of as being sickly if not actually dying: the dramatic, the anxiety-producing activities are those of the federal government. The mundane, the commonplace are handled by state and local units. The issues of burning controversy often are those decided by the federal government, though this is by no means always the case. (There is little to equal the battles that can be fought over proposed racial integration for the public schools, new curriculum for the grade school, or a new zoning ordinance for the city.) Yet, how can we compare subdivision restrictions with foreign-aid proposals as issues for generating political heat? How can the question of future water needs compare in emotional impact with that of whether or not the United States should recognize the government of Red China? How can we compare the amenities of the consumer (recreation, health, or street-lighting policies) with the problems of the citizen as a wage earner (labor relations rules, provisions for old age)?

This difference in dramatic appeal is largely related to the fact that, as citizens, we are all anxious and fearful concerning foreign commitments and the state of our defenses. If we consider only the domestic programs of American governments, this differential advantage is less obvious. The struggles over school integration, federal grants-in-aid programs, and how much subsidy to give the faltering railroads are often filled with controversy, but these battles do not gain more attention than some of the conflicts over state and local policies, conflicts related to questions of adding to the local school plant or the adoption of a water fluoridation ordinance, for example.

The federal government, indeed, performs few domestic functions on an exclusive basis; the operation of the postal system and old age and survivors insurance ("social security") are unusual exceptions. It strongly affects policy, however—particularly in the innovative phases where conflict is most acute—and has major financial responsibility in the areas of protecting our natural resources, in nonhighway transportation (such as in the subsidizing of air and water shipping), in some areas of business and labor regulation, and in the interpretation of civil rights. Housing, urban renewal, and public welfare (including antipoverty programs) are shared about equally, in terms both of policy making and of financing, by federal and state-local governments. In most other areas of domestic governmental policies, the state or local units, or the two acting jointly, dominate.[1]

THE EXPANSION OF STATE AND LOCAL PROGRAMS

GRANDFATHER'S DAY AND OURS On the frontier, a man was on his own. He could expect little help from government, and the work that had to be done—clearing the forests, breaking up the prairie, founding new towns—required mostly the pioneers' personal sweat and muscle. State government, furthermore, seemed almost as distant from him as the European capitals, for existing means of transportation and communication in a vast land limited the usefulness of state government as a problem-solving institution in the realm of social action. The rise of state government and the expansion of local government beyond record keeping and minimal services in the fields of roads, welfare, and education are largely products of the last two generations. They stem, in other words, from the age of the automobile, the telephone, and the interdependent, specialized economy of an urban rather than a rural society.

---

[1] See U.S. Bureau of the Census publications and the most recent edition of *Facts and Figures on Government Finance,* published biennially by the Tax Foundation, Inc., New York.

In 1913, all state governments taken together spent only 297 million dollars. In the two generations since that time and even allowing for the declining value of the dollar, state expenditures have increased twentyfold and local expenditures nearly sixfold.

In 1913, states spent little money for schools, except for higher education. And relatively few persons went to college. Local governments provided much of the education of the day through the one-room school, offering minimal programs taught by poorly trained and largely inexperienced teachers who received low pay. Teaching was regarded as a temporary occupation, not as a profession. Roads, another major expenditure program today, were largely cared for by the local unit two generations ago. They were often unsurfaced and required little care in that preautomobile age. Most states had little to do with highways before the beginnings of the good-roads movements and the adoption of the first federal-aid highway act (1916). The mentally ill received no rehabilitative treatment. They were given custodial care in ramshackle asylums run by untrained persons who received patronage appointments from the city, county, or state. Some patients were housed in the local jail. Welfare was a local function provided reluctantly, often in the county "poorhouse" at the bare subsistence level, and on the basis of a law first passed in England in 1601; the states were not involved at all, except for some institutional care.

State-government functions were simple in structure and few in number, for the most part. They centered around the regulation of utilities and other business, control over the state colleges and universities, enactment of the laws governing commercial transactions and the criminal statutes, and supervision over local government powers and activities. Local government was more active and spent more than state government—about 6.6 times as much—but was a thin shadow of its present self as a supplier of services to the citizen.

The picture of what has happened in two generations is quite clear—there has been a vast expansion of services, and state activities have expanded at a greater rate than have local governments. The latter have come to depend more and more upon the states for financial assistance, for the state governors and legislators have generally preferred to keep control over financial resources and to give assistance through grants-in-aid or shared taxes rather than through expanded tax bases for local governments. Furthermore, certain functions that were once principally the responsibility of some local unit have been or are being transferred to the states. Thus, the states are financing (with the federal government) most of the cost of public welfare, once exclusively a local function. Similarly, water and air pollution problems cannot be handled effectively at the local level and are being accepted as state responsibilities, increasing amounts of highway mileage are being turned over to the state by counties and cities, and the states are rapidly expanding their contributions to primary and secondary education, once financed entirely out of local property taxes paid to the school district.

All these figures indicate an increasing financial superiority on the part of states in relation to their local subdivisions. They indicate that we can expect an increasing amount of lobbying by local government officials before state legislatures and that the state governments will become more and more the political battleground for the resolution of many financial problems relative to local services. Whether the increasing trend toward state financing of services will also be reflected in increasing state domination over policy making is a matter for speculation and for research which has, up to now, not been done. To date, state aid has been chiefly in the nature of shared revenues with no strings attached—local elective officers and party officials have had sufficient influence to keep state supervision at a minimum.

REASONS FOR THE SOCIAL SERVICE STATE Much political discussion today centers around the question of what the extent of state and local services "ought" to be. Opinions are sometimes stated in terms of how high taxes "ought" to be, with little relating of taxes to services and other activities of government. Both "high" taxes and government "interference" in our everyday activities are sometimes denounced as if they exist in spite of what citizens want. It is true that probably no individual citizen wants *all* of the services government provides or is in favor of helping to pay for all of them. Government service levels do expand in part as the result of pressures from the bureaucracy which seeks to move governmental agencies toward the standards and goals established by professional groups, such as engineers, public health physicians, educators, and others. And interest groups do demand services in their own particular areas of concern without considering the effect of these demands upon the total cost of government, upon the relationship of service wants to existing revenue sources or the necessity for a tax increase, or of the nonmonetary costs that go along with some benefits that are demanded—such as the need to give up free choice in the use of land if citizens wish to have attractive cities, efficiently geared to the economy they are intended to serve. Yet, the important fact is that *government service levels have expanded over the past two generations principally as the result of demands from citizens who see government as the best available medium for helping them to meet problems that emerge in a constantly more complicated urban, industrial social system.* Whether these demands have been desirable, logical, rational, or fair is an ideological question that the author, as a political scientist, is not equipped to answer. He can only explain what has happened and why. He cannot scientifically evaluate its desirability, though as a citizen, he has personal values and hence preferences.

THE COMING OF THE SOCIAL SERVICE STATE   What kinds of changes have taken place over the past two generations? How have they affected state and local activities? Space permits only the briefest answer here.[2] The first effective nonbusiness demands for action came from farmers. Although they are vaunted in American folklore as the true "rugged individualists," they were actually the first major segment of the society to demand collective action. The Granger movement, beginning in the 1870s, sought legislation to regulate the railroads and marketing facilities upon which farmers were dependent. The land-grant college movement that resulted from the Morrill Act of 1862 represented one of the first federal-state cooperative programs and the Smith-Lever Act of 1914 was a bellwether later followed by many urban interest groups. It established the agricultural extension service which put a "county agent" into almost every county in the nation to serve as a "free" consultant to farmers. Significantly, the program was paid for jointly by federal, state, and county tax funds, and policy for the service was made cooperatively by the three levels of government.

[2] A fuller development may be found in Charles R. Adrian, *State and Local Governments,* 3d ed., McGraw-Hill Book Company, New York, 1971, especially chap. 2.

The farmer was only the first to seek to improve his economic position and reduce his insecurities through government. As people moved into the cities, leaving the farm in favor of gaining greater opportunities for advancement, they also began to realize the need for advanced education in a complicated society. Where children had left school early when their goal was to become farmers, they now wanted to continue their education beyond eight grades, or their parents wanted them to do so. Twelve grades of schooling became the standard. In 1890, more than 93 percent of the children of high school age were not in a school of any kind. Eighty years later, more than 80 percent of them were in school and the figure was still rising. The simple curriculum of the frontier was no longer adequate for a day of elaborate machines, electronic computers, and technicians of every sort. The schools had to teach those who wanted a vast variety of skills, as well as those who wanted to prepare for entering fine colleges and universities. At the same time parents, who had viewed children as an economic asset on the farm, saw them as a liability in the city, unwanted in idleness around their small homes or apartments. On the farm, child labor had been considered acceptable, indeed necessary for the development of firm character. In the city, however, it was considered dangerous, a threat to health, morals, and wage levels. It is now generally prohibited by law. The impact upon school systems and school costs resulting from these changes has been enormous. The corresponding demand for higher education, once restricted largely to the aristocracy and the wealthy, had an almost equal impact upon state government.

URBANISM AND THE STATE Other changes profoundly altered the way of life that our ancestors were accustomed to, and some of them were almost as expensive as the changes that took place in the field of education. The farmer or small-town dweller could, before World War I, meet most of his own health, economic, and psychological needs. An urban society, however, was totally different. Where great numbers of people lived in close proximity, water and sewage were both matters of prime public health consideration. Ultimately, the only safe way to protect people's health was through providing carefully engineered—and expensive—physical plants to supply water and to dispose of sewage. Again it was government that could best handle the situation; certainly it was unthinkable for the individual to do it alone. Houses became more expensive and smaller—there was no longer room for retired parents, widowed sisters, or orphaned nephews. Relatively few people found that they could provide adequately for their own retirement independently of their children. Yet the children too often could afford neither to feed nor house their parents. And even the elderly person who was willing to work found that there were no jobs to be had—he was "too old."

Illness or injury now spelled economic disaster to the factory worker or the white-collar clerk whose pay offered little opportunity for saving. Certainly friends or relatives could not take over the job for him temporarily. Unemployment of an involuntary nature became not merely a potential threat—it became commonplace. A man who worked for an impersonal corporation might be laid off at any time for any number of reasons not of his own making. The destruction of the environment through overcrowding could not be avoided by voluntary cooperation. Only government could hope to do the job.

Urban society, therefore, produced economic interdependence where independence had once existed. It produced insecurities nearly unknown in an agrarian society. These circumstances caused people to look around for a social institution to help them regain the poise and security that had slipped away from them. The most likely candidate—perhaps the only one available, in fact—was government.

NEW SERVICE DEMANDS There were dozens of other differences between a rural and an urban society that altered the social functions of government. The disappearance of the "ole' swimmin' hole" and of the family farm's picnic grove produced demands for recreation functions—and these demands were sharpened by the increasing leisure time of a wealthy nation. The strains created by the harsher pressures of urban life and work added to the need for facilities to care for the mentally ill; and medical advancements and changing social values created demands that such persons not merely be kept in custody, but that they be treated while in state hospitals. The fears and insecurities of ghetto life produced demands for the alleviation of poverty.

Automobiles produced demands for highways and for parking facilities. The multifold uses of land in an urban nation as compared with the simple patterns in a nation of yeoman farmers and the resultant conflicts created calls for land-use controls. The same thing was true of water. Someone had to allocate its uses to the many human activities that demanded it and someone had to keep the sources of supply reasonably free of pollution. Urban life meant interdependent economies rather than individual farming. For a time in the nineteenth century, the nation followed the same rules of *laissez faire* for business and industry that it used for farming, but gradually demand came for increased regulation just as it had for increased services. For example, the careless use of natural resources produced a reaction in an elaborate conservation program. A man found that it was one thing to trust his friend, the small-town merchant, another to deal with the large, impersonal firms of the city. Industry could at one time do largely as it pleased, but as the percentage of the population that was made up of urban working people increased, so did the political force of working-class people who expressed dissatisfaction with existing wages, hours, and conditions of labor. They began to demand regulation of industry, as well as security against total dependence upon it for existence. Each change in life style, each new problem, produced demands for action by government, and a great number of the new activities became the responsibilities of state and local governments.

REVENUES AND EXPENDITURES

STATE AND LOCAL BUDGETS How these various demands for increased governmental services and regulations have been met by state and local governments, and how they have affected government budgets have varied widely from state to state and from one locality to another. Each reader will have to do a bit of research for himself in his own state and community, for the patterns differ widely according to differing life styles, economic bases, rural urban population distributions, and dominant cultural and political values. New York and New Jersey are both Eastern, urban, industrial states with populations drawn largely from the same streams of immigration and migration, yet New York provides for elaborate state programs and grants-in-aid to local governments in virtually every area of domestic program activities known in America, while New Jersey's state government operates at what is perhaps the minimum level of operations possible in an urban, industrial state. New York's governors, whether Republican or Democratic, have over the years provided powerful and effective leadership for the expansion of state activities; New Jersey's governors

TABLE 1 Direct general expenditures by level of government, 1967 (millions of dollars)

	FEDERAL	STATE	LOCAL
National defense and international relations	74,638		
Education	2,295	9,384	28,534
Highways	100	9,423	4,510
Natural resources	7,810	1,801	542
Health and hospitals	3,227	3,358	3,283
Public welfare	1,374	4,291	3,927
Housing and urban renewal	944	28	1,441
Air transportation	860	65	400

Source: U.S. Bureau of the Census, *Compendium of Government Finances,* 1969, Table 7.

over the same period have nearly all offered what one disenchanted citizen of that state once called "dynamic nonleadership." Similar contrasts could be drawn between Oregon and Washington, Texas and Louisiana, and many other states, as well as between communities that lie close to one another physically.

We can generalize about where state and local governments are putting their funds, however. Broadly speaking, the most expensive activities are those of education, highways, public health (especially mental health), and public welfare, at the state level, and education, highways, public welfare, and sanitation, at the local levels (see Table 1). Of course, the power and importance of government cannot be judged solely on the basis of the size of its budget. Local government exercises significant influence over our everyday activities through its police powers and land-use controls (zoning, subdivision, and building-construction codes), for example. State governments regulate utilities, banks, and insurance companies, license professional practitioners, and define criminal activity, among a great many other things.

STATE AND LOCAL REVENUES As might be expected of a society growing increasingly dependent upon government for the performance of services, state and local revenue yields have grown enormously in the twentieth century. Sources of these revenues have become considerably diversified.

While state and local revenue totals increased about seventy-five times between 1902 and 1963, some increases have been even more spectacular. Thus, state and local liquor store receipts were a mere 2 million in 1902 but were 1,665 million dollars in 1967. There were no general state sales taxes at all in 1902, and this source produced only 499 million dollars in 1940. But in 1967 it brought 10,124 million dollars in state revenues. The state personal income tax was also nonexistent at the beginning of the century. It produced only 206 million dollars in 1940 but had reached 5,826 million dollars by 1967 and was widely regarded as the tax most likely to expand in the future. Other tax sources untapped at the beginning of the century but which are now important producers of revenue include the motor fuel, motor vehicle, cigarette, severance (removal or consumption of natural resources), and corporate income taxes and unemployment compensation insurance charges. The general property tax, which produced more than 50 percent of state tax revenues in 1902, had declined in importance by 1967 to such an extent that it accounted for only 1.4 percent of revenue at that level.

Local governments received 73 percent of their tax revenues from the general property tax in 1902. This figure had declined to 51 percent in 1967. Yet, the dollar increase in property tax collections during this period amounted to more than a twentyfold rise. Personal income and especially sales tax receipts had become important for local governments, as had utility and liquor store profits.

As compared with the beginning of the twentieth century, the most impressive change in local receipts has been in the growth of state grants and shared taxes. Local governments received less than 6 percent of their total revenue from state intergovernmental payments in 1902; this had increased to about 25 percent in 1950 and has remained approximately the same since. Federal direct grants have increased in importance, too, but at a far smaller rate than the attention paid to them would indicate. In 1902, 0.4 percent of local revenues came from federal grants; in 1964, this percentage had increased to 2.8. Major trends indicate a development of the sales tax as the principal expanding source of income for governments at local levels.

TAX SOURCES All taxes are ultimately derived from either of two sources: property or income. Taxes are theoretically based upon some criterion of ability to pay, although the criteria used in various periods of history have not been the same, and a tax created in one period and logical and equitable at that time may be continued into another era when its justification becomes less apparent. In some instances, payments to the government are based upon a benefit theory rather than on ability to pay, but such payments are more in the nature of service charges than of taxes. The benefit theory is used, for example, in cases of special assessments for street, sidewalk, street lighting, and similar improvements. There is another strong tradition which holds that all persons have an equal obligation to pay taxes. This argument makes it right for the government to collect taxes as involuntary contributions. It is also used, especially by conservatives, as a basis for holding that every adult should participate in the payment of a major tax. The theory would thus reject a personal income tax which exempted low-income persons.

LIMITS ON TAXING Local governments have only those powers of taxation that are granted to them by the state. The only exceptions to this rule are to be found in a few states, notably California and Wisconsin, where court interpretations of a constitutional home-rule clause have given cities a general grant of powers to levy taxes. The taxing powers of local governments are ordinarily limited either through the constitution or state statutes. The states often impose conditions and regulations on the administration of local finances.

States, too, are limited as to taxation. Most of their constitutions place limits of one kind or another on legislative taxing powers. The courts tend to hold to a narrow interpretation of authorizations to tax, and although state legislatures are less restricted than are local governing bodies, they are not left entirely free to decide taxing levels.

LIMITATIONS ON SUBJECTS OF TAXATION The subjects that may be taxed by local governments are normally strictly controlled by the state. Nearly all of the states tell their local governments which taxes they may levy, for what period of time they may be levied, and under what conditions. A local government that finds its property tax consistently inadequate may not, for example, decide to levy a payroll or a sales tax. The state must first authorize such a levy on a new subject.

The state government is also frequently limited as to the subjects that may be taxed. The constitution may prohibit the state from levying certain kinds of taxes or may limit the amount of the tax. Some states are thus restricted on the use of property, income, and sales taxes.

THE CONCEPT OF EQUITY   Legislators, when they plan long-range tax policies, must consider both adequacy and equity. "Equity" is usually thought of as meaning ability to pay. In colonial America, ability to pay could best be measured in terms of property or total wealth. Today, when most people receive a regular pay check (unlike the situation in the predominantly agricultural colonies), income is generally considered by economists to be a better criterion.

The income tax takes into consideration the fact that not all property is equally taxable. A home, most Americans would hold, is less suitable for taxation than is a factory. A factory that is losing money is less a subject for taxation than one that is making a profit (although it could be argued that it should pay some taxes nonetheless). The property tax makes them pay equally, the income tax does not. The income tax, in a complicated modern world, can be more equitably administered and is less subject to evasion than is the property tax.

THE GENERAL PROPERTY TAX   Despite the fact that the property tax has been bitterly attacked in recent years as being unsuitable for a modern and especially an urban society, it remains by far the most important source of revenue for local government. This is especially true of local units other than cities and school districts. The former are succeeding to some extent in diversifying their tax base, while the latter are becoming increasingly dependent upon state and federal aid.

The general property tax was the principal source of income for state governments from colonial times until the Great Depression. In the 1930s, tax delinquencies were common, the states needed better sources of revenue, and the whole of the property tax, to the extent that it could be collected, was needed by local governments. The result was that the states shifted to income and sales taxes. Most states no longer make a general levy at all.

Objections to the tax are many. It has already been suggested that it is no longer a very good measurement of ability to pay and is hence inequitable. It is often poorly administered and is in any case difficult to administer.

WHY IS THE PROPERTY TAX RETAINED? Many problems are connected with the property tax, but it continues to be the backbone of local government finance for a number of reasons. These include inertia (property taxpayers prefer assessment by neighbors and have often rejected proposals to put assessment on a professional basis) and the venerable argument holding that any old tax is a good tax and any new tax is bad. This argument is at least partly valid, for society has accommodated itself to an old tax, but a new one causes much uncertainty as to who will bear the actual burden of it.

The property tax is also one of the few taxes whose subjects will stay put. Most real property (if not personal property) is not easily moved out of the taxing jurisdiction. Sales taxes on the local level tend to drive shoppers and buyers out of the taxing jurisdiction. Taxes upon income tend to cause political complications if levied upon nonresidents and if not, tend to drive homeowners, businesses, and industry outside the jurisdiction. The property tax is also retained because it produces a very high yield, except in severe depressions. Local units of government are badly in need of money, and no one has suggested a substitute satisfactory enough to replace the tax. Cities in particular, among local units, have tried to ease the burden upon the property owner by diversifying the tax base through the addition of other taxes. These have served to supplement rather than replace the basic tax, however.

THE SEARCH FOR NEW SOURCES As noted above, the states largely withdrew from the general property tax field during the Great Depression. If there was ever a possibility of their reentering this field, it disappeared with the rapid increases in local government costs. In looking for a foundation for their tax systems, most of the states turned to a broad-based sales tax. This proved to be a fortunate choice as far as raising revenue in difficult times was concerned. Because it ordinarily applies to all retail transactions including necessities such as food and fuel, the tax yields relatively well in both depression and boom times. After watching the general sales tax returns of their neighbors, one state after another adopted the tax until by 1967, 43 states used it in one version or another.

Some states, as the result of the demands of local political forces, adopted the personal or corporate income tax or both, rather than the sales tax. Generally, however, these taxes appeared as supplements to the sales tax. In 1971, 41 states levied a personal income tax. The same number of states had corporation income taxes. Of the states with a broad sales tax, 44 also levied corporate income taxes, and 29 had personal income taxes. Twenty-eight states had all three of these major taxes, although the rates of each varied a good deal.

The trend has been toward increasing existing taxes and the imposition of both sales and personal income taxes at the state—and sometimes also the local—level of government. The picture has been complicated by increasing urbanization and the need to finance metropolitan-wide urban services.

REVIEW QUESTIONS

1. In general, what types of activities do American state and local governments engage in?

2. Why do federal government activities generally attract more public attention than do those of state and local governments?

3. Discuss the reasons for the rise of the "social service state."

4. In what ways has the coming of industrial, urban society affected the function of government in American society?

5. Why do the types and levels of governmental services differ from one state to another?

6. What are the principal sources of state revenues?

7. What are the principal sources of local revenues?

8. What are some of the criticisms levied against the general property tax? Why is it nevertheless retained?

9. What is meant by equity in taxation? How equitable is the tax system of your state, city, and school district?

10. What kinds of limitations on local taxation exist in your state? How are the limitations imposed?

3 STATE EXECUTIVES AND ADMINISTRATION

Throughout history, both in democratic nations and under other forms of government, leadership has come from the administrators of government, and particularly from the chief executive. This historic fact has sometimes been obscured by the doubts that Americans have always had about both chief executives and professional bureaucracies. These doubts began with the conflicts that existed between colonial assemblies, representing the people who had voted for their membership, and the governors of the colonies, most of whom held office by appointment from the British Crown.

This attitude of skepticism lived on after the War for Independence, in part because it was suited to the individualism that was characteristic of a frontier society. Throughout the nineteenth century, the powers of executives in public office were carefully circumscribed and balanced with a system of checks. The increasing complexity of government in the twentieth century has brought with it a demand for more effective leadership. This, in turn, has resulted in a trend toward increasing the power of the chief executive at all levels of government. In some cases this trend has been rapid (as in cities), in other cases slow (as in counties and states), but overall it has existed for each type of government.

THE CONFLICT OVER CENTRALIZED LEADERSHIP

The question of how much power to give the chief executive has in Europe historically been intertwined with the conflict between the elements of society, especially the commercial interests, which stood to profit from central regulation, and other people whose interests were best served by the maximization of government decision making at the local level. This was the case at the time of the American War for Independence. Through much of our history, however, it has been the commercial and industrial interests that have opposed federal regulation and the increase of the powers of the executive, and that have favored "states rights." Businessmen early became aware that in many areas state regulation may be depended upon to be weak and ineffective. The small farmer (and the small-town merchant) disliked central government whether it was in the hands of the king or of the leaders of the larger businesses and of industry. He correctly perceived that an increase in executive power is likely to be an instrument for centralization. Only with the advent of the social service state, during the Great Depression, did the strengthening of the executive become a generally popular cause, and even then it was the result of desperation.

Although the Jacksonian period saw some increase in the general status of chief executives and a rise from the low esteem of the period just after the War of Independence, those dominant in politics during the first half of the nineteenth century also kept executives weak by favoring rotation in office, many elective positions, short terms, and a romantic view of grass-roots government. The Jacksonians represented the worker and the yeoman farmer, not the commercial interests of the day, and they reflected the values of these groups.

THE "WEAK" GOVERNOR In the years following the Civil War, party responsibility, which had served to coordinate the activities of the many elective officers, broke down. However, most Jacksonian traditions, including those of rotation in office, amateurism, the long ballot, and others, remained. The result was a highly diffused executive power. During this period, the standards of morality in business and society generally permitted corruption to become widespread. When reformers began to make their influence felt in the 1870s and afterward, they favored taking many governmental activities "out of politics" by establishing them outside the regular political structure. The result was an increase in the number of independent boards and commissions. By the beginning of the twentieth century, the typical state governor was administratively impotent, unless as boss or through the party machine he could achieve the powers the law denied him.

After about 1910, a move for increasing the powers of the chief executive began to have some effect. The reasons for the development of an executive head include the trend toward increasing complexity of government, making coordination more urgently necessary; the high cost of modern government, which encouraged many citizens to grasp at any possibility for cutting down expenses; and the increasing prestige of executives together with a growing conviction that the people could elect someone who would act, not for the barons of industry, but for the "common man." The increased administrative and legislative influence of the governor helped attract able persons to the job and this acted, in turn, to increase the status of governors. Modern advances in the art of administration made it possible to bring the efforts of a vast number of people to a single focus in the office of the chief executive. Urbanization had an effect upon the governor and his office, for he became increasingly the spokesman for the larger cities, protecting the urbanite from the potential hostility of legislatures dominated by rural and small-town dwellers. The Great Depression helped add to the prestige of executives at all levels of government when citizens turned to firm leadership in a social service state as the best hope for a cure for their personal economic problems and insecurities.

FORCES FOR SEPARATISM State government policies have not generally been guided by an overall concept of purpose and goal. Unlike
some local governments that have policies quite coherently aimed at
boosterism or the provision of certain consumer amenities, or at some
other image of the "proper" end of government, state policies have
tended to be the result of compromise. Each interested group in the
state political process seeks to maximize its own influence over policy
in part by striving for the independence of the agencies in which it has
an interest. Therefore, state government reorganization along the lines
of the corporation with its integrated administration has been slow.
This has been in contrast to cities, where the civic leaders have often
favored integration, have made it part of their program of municipal
action, and have had enough influence to achieve their goals.

Nearly all the "Little Hoover Commission" studies that were conducted in about one-half of the states in the early 1950s placed heavy
emphasis upon administrative integration along the lines advocated by
the efficiency and economy movement of a generation earlier. These
groups generally argued for the following: (1) use of the short ballot
and concentration of authority and responsibility in the governor;
(2) reduction in the number of departments to perhaps a dozen or so;
(3) elimination of boards from administrative responsibilities; (4) development of a cabinet and personal staff for the governor; (5) provision
for an independent audit of state funds made to the legislature; (6) development of a personnel system based upon merit principles; and
(7) preparation of a budget and controlled expenditure of funds under
the supervision of the governor.[1] Administrative reorganization movements are discussed further in a companion volume in this series.[2]

The lack of a unified purpose for the states in terms of substantive
policies has reenforced a number of other factors opposing integrated
administration:

1. Agencies prefer a maximum of autonomy. A department head may
claim, with interest-group representatives in emphatic agreement, that

---

[1] The classic statement of the arguments for these reforms may be found in
A. E. Buck, *The Reorganization of State Governments in the United States,*
Columbia University Press, New York, 1938.

[2] John J. Corson and Joseph P. Harris, *Public Administration in Modern Society,* McGraw-Hill Book Company, New York, 1963.

the placing of his agency under the chief executive or within a large department will result in a lower level of service to its clientele groups.

2. There is a strong tradition of separate responsibility to the electorate for many functions of government. Generally, most voters apparently prefer to elect an officer who has traditionally been elected, even when the functions of the officer are obscure. Much of the public apparently believes that direct election is more democratic than appointment by the governor; party leaders like to have several elective offices on the ballot so as to make it possible to "balance the ticket" geographically and ethnically.

3. The cleanup campaigns that follow scandals often result in recommendations that a particular function be "taken out of politics." In practice, this usually means that it is set up in a separate agency, and may be largely removed from gubernatorial control.

4. Clientele and interest groups normally prefer to have functions of their special concern separated from the rest of government. They also like to have separate or "dedicated" funds. Sportsmen, for example, prefer a small agency for fish and game to a vast agency including conservation, agriculture, and economic-development functions. Interest groups can more easily dominate policy under the former structure, which causes them to think in possessive terms, while the department head or the governor is more likely to do so under the latter. Citizens often favor the principle of "improved administration" but oppose specific proposals that would alter the existing pattern of operation of governmental functions in which they have interests.

5. Professional groups prefer separate organization for the functions that they regard as being a part of their profession. These groups have "organized bodies of knowledge," generally available only to members, group standards of training and performance, codes of ethical conduct, and, particularly, close group ties and associations.[3]

6. The strings attached to federal grants-in-aid encourage a link between federal and state administrators of particular functions (such as

[3]York Willbern, "Administration in State Governments," in *The Forty-eight States: Their Tasks as Policy Makers and Administrators,* The American Assembly, Graduate School of Business, Columbia University, New York, 1955, p. 116. This account borrows from Willbern's chap. 5.

public health), but they discourage the association of various state programs in a single agency.

7. Citizens and legislators often believe that certain kinds of programs are especially important and should exist in separate agencies apart from the regular political process. Liquor control and education are examples.

8. Legislators are reluctant to give greater power to the governor. Not only are they jealous of his glamour, political power, and policy leadership potential, but they often view him as the spokesman of the state's largest cities.

9. Many Americans have been skeptical of strong administrative leaders and have been more concerned with specific functions than with the abstract principle of efficient, well-coordinated government in general. Others believe that governors are not usually elected on the basis of issues and that it would be unwise to place all state activities under the direction of a man who must inevitably use campaign rather than professional criteria in making decisions.

THE ARGUMENTS FOR INTEGRATION Persons supporting reorganization have used two principal arguments to support their cause: that integration will produce coordinated governmental activities and that responsibility to the public will be increased. It is sometimes held that there is really not much to coordinate in state government, that there is little in common between the activities of the mental health department and the highway department. But reformers have argued in reply that coordination makes possible the economies of joint housekeeping activities and of the balancing off, in the executive budget, of the relative priorities of various functions of government. The chief executive is the only person available to perform the role of coordinator.

The argument on responsibility is based upon the assumption that there should be but a single legitimate source of authority, the chief executive, and that his lieutenants, the department heads, should receive their authority from him. Government, its services, and its many clientele groups are all too complicated for a simple, single line of responsibility, of course. Mose of those who would reorganize government recognize this, but they argue, according to Willbern, that "a general responsibility to the general public interest may be better achieved through the main line of political responsibility, focused on the legislature and the governor, than through the limited, specific, hidden responsibilities involved in some of the other relationships."

STATE AND FEDERAL ADMINISTRATION CONTRASTS AND REASONS
The Presidency and the federal administration descend from a tradition different from that of the states. The men who wrote the Constitution in 1787 were the leaders of trade and such industry as we then had. Such persons have historically favored effective government, controlled from some central pivot. They established a Constitution with administration centered in the President, for they wanted a government that could solve the problems that had been too much for the government under the Articles—one that had had few powers to start with, and that was administratively so structured that it could not be made effective.

While the President appoints (with Senate approval, which is seldom denied) virtually all department heads and can dismiss them at will, few governors have this power. The President's removal power is limited only in the case of judges and of the members of the so-called "independent regulatory commissions" (such as the Federal Power Commission), who can be removed only "for cause" which is usually specified in the law. These bodies are in theory independent of the President. They, in effect, write legislation in their particular fields. Except for these cases, and for the independence of a professional bureaucracy, the President is not only responsible for administration, but has enormous powers to control it through his selection and dismissal of top officeholders. Governors are far more restricted. Some state department heads are independently elected; they may not even be members of the same party as the governor, hardly a situation to encourage cooperation and a coordinated approach to policy. Some department administrators are appointed by someone other than the governor. In a few instances, they are chosen by the legislature. In many others they are chosen by a board or commission whose members may be elected, or may be appointed by the governor for overlapping terms. The latter arrangement requires a governor to be in power for a very long time in order to have a majority of his choices on the board. Usually he cannot remove members of boards except by some elaborate procedure. Sometimes removal is not in the hands of the governor at all, but rather in that of the state high court, civil service commission, or some other agency. The frequent result is that agencies headed by boards are dominated by the most powerful interest groups in the field of their responsibilities, or they may exist autonomously controlled by the bureaucracy and director of the agency. The governor, in any case, is not likely to have much influence over policies, except through the indirect device of budgetary control, and even then his budget may be rewritten by legislative leaders.

In some cases, governors must by law appoint a man from a slate presented to him by the principal interest groups concerned with an agency. Sometimes agencies are headed by ex officio boards made up of persons who are members because of some other office—often an elective one—that they hold. The pattern varies greatly. The most predictable thing about it is that, except for a very few states which have moved toward the federal government's integrated organization, the governor is not likely to have effective control over state agencies.

THE GOVERNOR VERSUS THE LONG BALLOT   Except in a few states (notably Alaska, New Jersey, New York, Tennessee, and Virginia), the governor serves more as first among equals than as the head of administration. He must negotiate with other state elective officials who are actually his colleagues, who may be of a different party or faction, and who may have secured their elections perhaps as part of his team, but possibly independently of him both as to nomination and election. Sometimes, as in Iowa, Michigan, and West Virginia, these independent officials are brought together for certain statutory purposes as a board and become a plural executive. The board may have many of the powers which, on the federal level, would rest with the Chief Executive.

The most common elective position is that of the lieutenant governor (39 states), who often serves ex officio on a variety of boards. Others commonly elected are the secretary of state, attorney general, treasurer, auditor, and members of various boards and commissions, especially for highways, public instruction, and higher education.[4] It should not be assumed that these officers are not often of consider-

---

[4] For details, see the latest volume of the *Book of the States,* Council of State Governments, Chicago.

able influence in policy making, even though many of their duties are routine. The attorney general has an opportunity to gain headlines by investigating irregularities, graft, and corruption. He can often decide what he is going to investigate and hence whose ox is to be gored. He is the chief interpreter of the law and chief law-enforcement officer of the state. Legislative acts are not self-defining, and his office spends a great deal of time preparing opinions concerning the powers of various state agencies, of local governments, and even of the governor—opinions which sometimes come out of the process with interpretations not unfavorable to the political interests of the attorney general and of his party or faction.

The secretary of state's ordinary duties include the keeping of the official records. He also generally acts as the returning officer for elections and may have some supervisory powers in this connection. As such, he may be able to expedite or delay special elections as political considerations dictate. Because he may dominate the state board of canvassers, some secretaries in the past have been suspected of helping to "count out" an unwanted candidate in a close election.

The auditor is supposed to check up on the administrative branch of government. Often he performs accounting functions, although the trend is toward placing these in a finance department. Sometimes he has only the power of postaudit; that is, he reviews *after* the money is spent to see whether it was spent according to legislative intent (as he interprets it) and without corruption or undue waste. He (or the controller) may have the power of preaudit, or the right to approve expenditures *before* they take place. This enables him to interpret "legislative intent" and thus often to decide whether an agency is to be allowed to spend money for a certain purpose in a certain way—a most influential power. The auditor may also have discretionary powers over local governments that can affect the political fate of his party or faction; thus, he may be able to select the local governments whose books he is going to inspect, and he may try harder to find irregularities when inspecting in the camp of the enemy.

The treasurer is, in many ways, just an office manager. He can normally collect funds only according to state law which is interpreted by someone other than himself, and he can pay out moneys only on the order of the controller or auditor. Yet he can have considerable influence on public policy. He may decide, for example, which banks are to be favored with deposits of state money, and the amount of interest (if any) that the state will expect to be paid.

These men, individually and collectively, possess considerable power. Governors cannot ignore them. Even so, voters view the governor as the chief executive. In normal times, when anxiety levels are low, citizens want the powers of government to be widely dispersed; when they want action from the state, they sometimes expect things of the governor that may far exceed his legal powers. This set of conflicting attitudes is typical of American public opinion. But it is significant that the governor is thought of as the one best hope in time of troubles. And for that reason, his powers have been expanding in the twentieth century.

THE ROLES OF THE GOVERNOR

The governorship is many things, as is the Presidency, and the governor must play many social roles and must help the public to keep them individually identifiable. The governor is chief of state, the voice of the people, chief executive, commander in chief of the state's armed forces, chief legislator, and chief of his party.[5] No one man acting alone could play so many roles. He must have a staff to assist him, yet it is necessary that the public see him as doing the job alone. The play requires him to act out all of the parts, he must appear (if he wishes to be effective in the office) to be all-seeing and all-knowing, at least to be aware and have an understanding of every matter that the public and the press expects him to be informed on and have an opinion about.

The governorship must be viewed as an institution. The chief executive loses, during much of his official day, his individual personality and becomes part of the total institution—the governorship. It consists of not only the governor, but also his personal staff, certain other high government officials (who may be organized as a cabinet), and the principal members of his political party or of his faction of it. The governor may or may not be the actual leader of the team. Publicly, of

[5] These categories follow those in Clinton Rossiter, *The American Presidency,* Harcourt, Brace & World, Inc., New York, 1956.

course, he is the entire institution. His supporters and the public generally are unaware of most of the other members.

CHIEF OF STATE Like the President, though in a much more modest way, the governor serves as the living symbol of the state. In his role, he is not a representative of a political party. He is not seen as the man who controls patronage or struggles with the legislature over a new state school-aid formula. Instead, he is the representative of all of the people of the state and perhaps of all society, as he dedicates a new highway, or opens the state convention of the Sea League of America, or throws out the first baseball of the season, or sends greetings to the Western Bohemian Fraternal Association.

He is called upon to shake hands with thousands of convention members as they visit the state capital, and he shakes still more hands as he travels about the state by automobile and airplane. Though much of the work—the proclamations, the letters, the speeches—can be taken care of by the staff, the rituals, both sacred and profane, which the governor is expected to take part in require much of his personal time. He avoids them at genuine peril to his political career. Most governors welcome the ceremonial functions, however, for they allow them to make contact with constituents under very favorable conditions and with a minimum of the tension and conflict that accompany appearance in the political role.

The governor is asked to send a letter of greeting to every kind of meeting, to issue a proclamation for every conceivable special day, week, or month. Of course, he cannot spend the necessary time to write such letters. Some long-suffering member of his staff must do that. But it is important that the letter or proclamation appear to be drafted by the governor himself and signed by him. Persons who would never consider voting for him will leave no telephone call unmade in their efforts to get a letter of greetings from the governor for the annual convention of their favorite organization. The governor is, after all, the living symbol of the state.

VOICE OF THE PEOPLE The governor is the spokesman for the morality, the higher aspirations, and the conscience of all the citizens of the state. While he is able to command only a small portion of the prestige and attention accorded to the President, he is still the only person in a position to speak of the ideals of the people of his state in a sense that is accepted as being "above politics." He becomes something of a father image, and in this role he talks of the need for more jobs, for "education for all," for the protection of the young and old, the dependent mother, the mentally ill. No matter what his policies may be, he is expected to present the higher values of society and to defend them—even though his means of implementing specific programs may belie his true interest in, say, the mentally ill, and although his detailed proposals may become items of intense controversy.

CHIEF EXECUTIVE   Although few governors have the legal powers necessary to make them masters over the way in which state agencies are administered, they do have numerous powers. Symbolically, they are regarded as at the head of the administration, and the governors' mail certainly indicates that they are so viewed by the public. As a political leader and as voice of the people, the governor may be able to exert influence over administration where his legal powers fail him. In many cases, however, the governor lacks both power and effective influence over the administration of some (perhaps many) departments, both because of the manner in which department heads are selected and because of legislative provisions designed to insulate certain agencies from gubernatorial influence.

APPOINTMENTS   Appointments made by the governor are generally subject to approval by the state senate, or by some other body, such as the House in Connecticut, both branches of the Virginia legislature, or the governor's council in three New England states. As was noted above, his appointing power is ordinarily greatly restricted. Even so, the typical governor has a very large number of positions to fill—several hundred, counting the various boards and commissions—and gubernatorial staffs have difficulty in keeping up with changes that take place.

The kind of person appointed varies with the interests of the governor and the pressures on him, and with the character of the position to be filled. Every state has a number of positions that do little to challenge the incumbent and which may be regarded as sinecures, but the number of these is declining.

American folklore seems to consider that "political appointments"— that is, those for non-merit-system positions—will be from among incompetent job seekers whose primary and perhaps only qualification is party loyalty and service. This was probably once the case, and the pattern now varies considerably from one state to another, but a contemporary governor cannot often afford to appoint "hacks" to critical positions—government performs too many important and complicated functions for him to risk his own political destruction by such folly. He is, however, subjected to pressures from party leaders who are often more interested in patronage than in effective administration and he must make some of his appointments in consideration of this pressure.

PERSONNEL ADMINISTRATION About 2.3 million persons worked for state governments in 1967. The number has increased over the years. More important, perhaps, is the fact that the jobs state employees perform are growing more complex each year.

In the last half of the nineteenth century, governmental jobs were often simple and the public did not expect them to be filled by professionally qualified persons. Demands for reform, beginning in the 1880s, and the changing requirements of the tasks of government produced the start of a trend toward a merit system for personnel. The states have been slower than the national government or the cities in adopting the merit principle—about one-half of the states still have no merit system at all, or the one they have applies to a very few agencies, generally those where federal grant programs make a merit system a condition of eligibility. Other states have merit systems for a considerable portion, but not all, of their employees. Several states have comprehensive merit systems. But even in states without a formal system based on merit, leaders must be concerned about the qualifications of appointees in the employee category just as they must be about department heads and other high-ranking officials.

Under the traditional patronage system, the governor and his party or faction were responsible for filling state positions. The usual practice—still followed in non-merit-system states—was for the governor to appoint a chief personnel officer who served on his staff. This man usually named a representative for each county whose task it was to handle regional appointments (such as those in the highway department) and to make recommendations for a proportionate share of the jobs at the capital. The governor thus had the power to choose which local faction of the party he would recognize and he could use patronage to consolidate his power and that of his faction. But he also had to umpire between conflicting party chieftains, a job that could earn him enemies, and to accept the consequences of appointments based on local party considerations rather than on qualifications for the job.

With the rise of the merit system, control over personnel was generally taken away from the governor. A civil service commission was usually established. Its members often served for long, overlapping terms and the law required them to be selected from more than one party in many cases. The commission was set up as something of a policeman, its task being to insulate state personnel from the political parties. It usually established elaborate rules for appointment and dismissal and a set of formal procedures designed to insure the insulation pattern. Civil servants, for example, were commonly forbidden to take part in political campaigns.

The independent commission plan was probably necessary in the early days of civil service reform because the administrative branch of government was often corrupt and opposed to the merit principle. But chief executives have since come to recognize more and more the advantage to them in having competent personnel who can help them compile a record of effective political action. With the emergence of this recognition, the negative or "policeman" approach to personnel administration became less important and in recent years there has been the beginnings of a trend toward the reestablishment of personnel controls in the hands of the governor. In private corporations, personnel management is invariably a task of top administration. It is an arrangement that is deemed necessary in order to assemble an effective working force. Much the same attitude is emerging in government. Recent trends in study commission reports have reflected the view that the governor needs more flexibility in his powers to appoint, promote, reassign, or dismiss state personnel. It seems likely that his powers in this area will expand in the future.

BUDGET CONTROL   During the 1920s and 1930s (earlier in a few states), economy pressures were so great that more than 40 state constitutions were amended to give the governor the power of the item veto over appropriations bills, and many legislatures surrendered part of their traditional power of control over the purse. Many reformers believed that pressures could be brought to bear on the governor to eliminate "pork barrel" provisions in appropriation bills and that the executive budget, which would have to be proposed to the legislature "in balance," would work toward the same end. They encouraged the establishment of all or part of the executive-budget system to replace the older arrangement under which budgets were never approached systematically, with the appropriations committees of each house, and often their subcommittees, determining the size of appropriations for various functions of government, and with two other committees determining taxes. Coordination was often extremely loose and the governor was sometimes virtually excluded from the budgetary process.

The executive-budget plan divides the financial process so that the executive branch makes a recommendation for revenues and expenditures in the form of a systematic, comprehensive statement of income and outgo. The legislature then adopts this budget, nearly always with some, and perhaps with many, modifications. The executive branch next oversees the expenditure of the appropriations by the various departments, requiring them to spend at a rate that will not exhaust their appropriations prematurely and will keep expenditures within the requirements of the law. In "emergencies," agencies may be permitted to spend at a greater rate than appropriations justify and then to apply for a deficiency or supplemental appropriation at the next legislative session. Finally, the legislative branch, through its auditors, checks to ascertain whether or not appropriate provisions of the state law have been followed by the executive. The power of the governor, through his budget officer, is potentially very great, both in preparing the budget itself—the document is, of course, a major policy statement, explaining how the governor would spend moneys—and in controlling its expenditure after the legislature votes the funds. The budget officer is, therefore, one of the governor's chief aides today. He and his budget examiners advise both the governor and legislators, reviewing appropriations requests and preparing evidence in support of the fiscal policy of the governor. He often controls the conditions under which the appropriations are spent.

CLEMENCY The pardoning power of the governor stems from the fact that he inherits some of the authority of the king in England. In feudal theory, the law was the monarch's; he could, therefore, pardon offenses against it. Until the twentieth century, the pardon was almost the only device whereby a convicted person could be released from prison short of the full term on his sentence. Once nearly 50 percent of all prisoners were pardoned.

The pardoning power was and still is sometimes abused. Among many examples that could be cited, there was Gov. John C. Walton of Oklahoma, who freed 693 prisoners in 11 months and was impeached and convicted (in 1923) for having taken bribes for some of the pardons. However, most governors have probably disliked the responsibility for acting on pardons and paroles. The decisions are difficult, and a serious mistake—releasing someone who then commits a headline-grabbing crime—can be politically costly. Decisions about prisoners under sentence of death are especially difficult.

Today, fewer than 2 percent of prison sentences are commuted and very few terminate in outright pardons, although in some states governors continue the tradition of granting a few pardons at Christmas time, a practice designed to help maintain morale among long-termers. Executive clemency now exists primarily to correct miscarriages of justice. It has been largely replaced by the use of parole, probation, and the indeterminate sentence; these devices have been turned over for administration to agencies of the state, with final decision in the hands of a parole board on which the governor may or may not sit and over which he has no veto.

COMMANDER IN CHIEF   The governor serves as commander in chief of the National Guard (state militia) when it is not called into national service, as it is in times of emergency or war. The Guard, which is largely supported by federal funds, has today apparently outlived its traditional function, but it is protected by powerful interest groups made up of members of the Guard and veterans' organizations. Before World War II, the Guard was used by the governor to handle large disturbances, such as prison riots, race riots, and strikes. In almost every case where it was used, the decision to do so provoked controversy.

Since World War II, the Guard has been used less and less to maintain order; that task is now frequently entrusted to state police or highway patrol forces, which are also generally under the governor's command and which are to be found in an increasing number of states. The Guard has, instead, become an instrument for rescue and relief. Guardsmen have assisted in all types of disaster relief, particularly in the wake of tornadoes, hurricanes, and floods. They have been used in recent years in many ghetto riots, but this is probably a stopgap measure. Guardsmen are not professional policemen. The National Guard as a military establishment seems outmoded. With its new functions it continues to be socially useful, but it is an expensive luxury.

CHIEF LEGISLATOR The typical citizen probably thinks of the governor not so much as an administrator as a policy leader. The governor has, in fact, become so important as a policy leader that the legislature's function in many, perhaps most, states, has become essentially negative in character. The legislature vetoes, modifies, or perhaps enlarges upon gubernatorial recommendations, but it is not likely to provide innovative policy leadership. The public does not seem to expect more than negative activity from the legislature. There are some exceptions to this, however. In a few states, governors have traditionally not been much concerned with issues of policy.

Legislative leaders often resist gubernatorial leadership and resent it, regardless of whether the governor is of their party or of another one. Yet the governor has the capacity to rally public opinion and to attract a great deal of publicity that can be useful in support of his recommendations. The very fact that he has superior public-relations power will be resented, however, as will the fact that he will often have an imaginative, varied program to present. These programs can be submitted with a good deal of public attention in budgets, regular and special messages to the legislature, and veto messages.

For purposes of policy innovation, the governor has great resources that are not so easily available to the part-time legislators. Because of the district system of election, the latter are more subject to grassroots, nonprofessional sentiment. Legislators and administrators are likely to see themselves as rivals. The governor is more likely to support the administrative agencies and to accept professional values and goals. He can call upon any of the state agencies for ideas and data, and even those in enemy or neutral hands cannot afford to refuse to give him the information he requests. He can also call upon knowledgeable people in private life for help. A favorite device is the study commission, often made up of persons who are politically inactive or of the opposite party, in addition to the governor's own support-ers. The legislature will sometimes refuse to appropriate money for such groups, but because of the prestige of a governor's study com-mission and of their interest in the subject matter, these people will often work hard without compensation or even payment of expenses. The ideas they develop are often immensely valuable to the governor and his staff in formulating a legislative program. (The commissions are sometimes appointed, of course, principally for the sake of delay or to take the pressure off the governor until he is ready to act or until no action is necessary. This is a different use for the same political institution, however.)

The rising importance of the governor as a policy leader has also increased his visibility as a target for the discontented. Demands in recent years for greater state expenditures in the costly areas of schools, roads, public welfare, and others, have often been accompa-nied by an insistence that the governor take a positive position on these issues. Where he has failed to meet the expectations of con-cerned groups, he may be punished by being denied reelection.

THE VETO   The power of veto is a great weapon in the hands of a governor. It is important both as a threat and in actual use. The veto is, incidentally, perhaps the only power possessed by governors that is generally broader in scope than the equivalent power of the President. The latter can veto whole bills as presented to him, but governors in all but nine states also have the item veto by which they can reject single sections of appropriation bills.

The Governor of North Carolina is the only one not possessing a veto. In other states, the strength of the veto power varies a great deal. The number of days which the governor is allowed to consider bills passed by the legislature varies from state to state. In all states, the legislature may override the governor's veto, usually by a two-thirds vote of the membership in both houses. Much legislation is passed during the closing days of a session, which sometimes give the governor an absolute veto, although in some states technical proce-dures have been devised to keep this power from him. There are great differences in the degree to which the veto is actually used.[6]

[6] For state-to-state differences in the veto power, see the most recent edition of the *Book of the States,* Council of State Governments, Chicago.

The power of the veto and the threat of its use lies in the fact that in most states it is very difficult to override one; the issue must usually be raised in the next political campaign, if it is to be raised at all. Not a single veto was overridden in Minnesota between 1858 and 1935, for example; only one in Pennsylvania in the first half of the twentieth century; and only four in Iowa in over a century.

CHIEF OF PARTY   The governor is the nominal, and frequently the real head of his political party. As such, he must spend a good deal of time attending party activities—barbecues, dances, picnics, rallies, and conventions. He must try to iron out disputes between rival factions within the organization or among rival members of the legislature. He must dispense patronage in a manner that preserves a reasonable level of satisfaction among the party rank and file, while at the same time securing persons for public office who will not embarrass him by their incompetence. A good appointment strengthens the hand of the governor and the standing of the party, but the low salaries and uncertain tenure that generally prevail make this difficult to accomplish.

In each election, the governor must get out and campaign for the party whether or not he is himself a candidate. As he travels about the state, he must make sure the local county chairman knows of his coming. A chairman who feels slighted may sit on his hands during the next campaign. When a United States senator dies or resigns, he must choose a successor who will be honored by party workers but not become a Frankenstein monster, stronger than the governor himself. He is expected to support the party platform, whenever he can determine what it means, and his voice in messages to the legislature is at once that of the governorship and of the party. His role as party leader, in fact, becomes intertwined with virtually everything he does, either explicitly or as a hidden purpose while he carries out his other duties.

THE BIG DECISIONS   In a sense, every decision made in the governor's office has important implications both for his political future and for the welfare of citizens, but some decisions are, of course, really critical for the governor or many citizens of the state. Some of these may have to be made under the pressure of time—a natural disaster, prison break, race riot, or an attention-getting move by the political opposition. Others may involve basic changes in public policy—new state programs, major alterations in the tax structure—but all are critical in nature. How are such decisions made? The answer probably varies with the personality of the governor, the political structure of the state, the alignment of interest groups, and other factors. The governor is likely to seek a wide range of opinions on the subject— from a citizens' committee if time permits, from his staff, the budget bureau, his major political supporters outside the party, party leaders, department heads, and others.

Finally, the governor alone, or perhaps a very small group of advisers together with the governor, will make the decision. It will be announced in a carefully timed and carefully worded press release. The party faithful will then be assisted in writing letters to the editor in defense of the decision. Legislative leaders will be briefed—few of them, if any, will have been on the inside in making the decision—so that they may use the "right" arguments. Reams of statistical evidence in support of the position will come from the budget office. Party chieftains will publicly praise the "courageous, imaginative leadership" of the governor. Ultimately the results, or what appear to be the results, of the decision will help to determine the political fate of the governor and of his party or faction. He cannot afford to be wrong often.

THE GOVERNOR'S STAFF If the governorship is an institution rather than the office of an individual, its brain-center is his personal staff. The staff in many states consists of no more than an executive secretary and clerical help, although in an increasing number of states it includes several professional persons in addition to stenographers, receptionists, file clerks, police aids, and telephone operators. The immediate staff is augmented by the person in charge of the executive budget and by political party leaders and the few paid members of the party staff.

Staff members must be persons of considerable ability who are willing to serve as alter ego to the governor. In the more populous states, the professional staff is likely to include persons serving as legal advisor, press secretary, patronage supervisor, legislative liaison officer, speech writer, and the like.

The staff is given an enormous number of responsibilities, but all of its work is presented to the public as that of the governor. It is he who must assume responsibility for it and the members must not attempt to claim personal credit if they wish to avoid damaging the governor's political career. The staff responsibilities include those of the development of policy recommendations to be presented to the public during campaigns and to the legislature during its sessions; public-relations activities designed to credit the governor with those things the voters consider to be good and to dissociate him from things considered bad; liaison with the various state, local, and federal agencies for which the governor may be responsible or which may be engaged in activities that may affect the governor's decisions; answering most of the governor's mail, creating good will toward him wherever possible and cutting red tape within state agencies on behalf of constituents when this can be done, or putting the writer in contact with someone who can help him; liaison with the legislature, so that the governor's legislative program can be furthered as much as possible; and liaison with the party, of which the governor is at least the nominal head, and with which the governor's political future is closely linked.

Much of the political success of a governor depends upon his own attractiveness to the voters, his stamina, and his drive, but he can possess what is needed in relation to all of these and still not be successful unless he can gather around him the types of staff members who can help him create the public image of one who "sees all, knows all" and has policy suggestions to make in connection with all of the things that are causing anxieties among a considerable number of voters.

LEGAL CONSIDERATIONS

In every state, usually in the constitution, regulations prescribe the qualifications for the governor. He must be a citizen of the United States. He must be of a certain age, usually at least 30. He must have lived in the state a certain period of time, usually at least five years, and he must be a qualified voter. These legal qualifications are generally far less important than are considerations of "availability," that is, whether a candidate is thought to command the public support necessary to be elected.

TERM OF OFFICE The early state constitutions commonly provided a one-year term for governors, but the trend has been toward longer terms. Massachusetts in 1920 was the last state to give up the one-year provision; and by 1971, 39 states had four-year terms. The others had two-year terms. In many states (especially in the South) a governor cannot succeed himself; in some others he can serve no more than two terms consecutively.

COMPENSATION AND PERQUISITES   The gubernatorial way of life is so costly that governors must be well paid, personally wealthy, or the recipients of gifts in order to meet the costs the job imposes. Governors must entertain legislators, visiting dignitaries, prominent citizens, and many others as a part of their normal duties. They must have large homes, and must dress in a manner suitable to their high status.

The Governor of Arkansas, in 1968, was the lowest-paid state chief executive, receiving $10,000 per year. Eight of the most populous states paid $40,000 or more. Most governors received $25,000 or less. To be sure, they receive a good deal of pay in terms of prestige, and they also are entitled to various perquisites. Many states furnish the governor a home, usually called a "mansion," sometimes also a summer home, an automobile or two (with state police bodyguard-chauffeur), the use of an airplane when on anything that can possibly be classified as "state business," and other material things and privileges.

REMOVAL AND SUCCESSION   In addition to death, resignation, or the assumption of residence outside the state, governors may be removed by conviction on impeachment (except in Oregon), and this has happened on ten occasions. Impeachment is a convenient political weapon, and almost every governor who attempts to provide legislative leadership will be threatened with its use, though the threat is seldom carried out. The usual procedure is for the lower house to institute impeachment proceedings on the basis of charges involving mis-, mal-, or nonfeasance in office, that is, use of the office in an improper, criminal, or neglectful manner. The trial on the impeachment usually takes place in the senate; the penalty on conviction is removal from office. Additional penalties may be imposed, and the governor, once out of office, may be tried in the regular courts if criminal charges are made.

One governor, Lynn Frazier of North Dakota, was recalled from office by a vote of the people (1922). This device is authorized in several states but is rarely used, the process being complicated and expensive because of the large number of petition signatures required.

If the governor leaves office, his successor, in 38 states, is the lieutenant governor. In states that have no such officer, or if that office is vacant, a designated administrative or legislative officer succeeds to the office. Unlike the practice in the federal government, the designated successor acts for the chief executive whenever the latter leaves the state.

REVIEW QUESTIONS

1. Why is American tradition opposed to centralized administrative leadership?

2. What is meant by a "weak" governor?

3. What forces have encouraged "separatism" in state administration?

4. Explain why "integrated" administration has tended to accompany the trend toward expanded state and local activities.

5. Discuss the differences in state and federal administration and the reasons for these.

6. Explain why city governments are more likely to have integrated administrative structures than are state governments.

7. What has been the effect of the long ballot upon the powers of the governor? Explain why.

8. Give an example of the governor of your state in each of the roles of his office. Use actual news stories as sources.

9. What are the advantages to the governor of having a professional staff?

10. How may the governor of your state be removed from office?

4 STATE LEGISLATURES

How does a legislator spend his time? Debating the momentous issues of his generation? Studying the basic social and economic facts that shape the policies of his state? Thinking up brilliant solutions to problems that have been plaguing the people? Making "a play for a spot in the history books" by standing fiercely on principle in the face of the "selfish" demands of interest groups? Probably not, unless he is a very unusual person.

The late Richard L. Neuberger, a journalist who was elected to the Oregon legislature (and later to the United States Senate), put it this way: "A member of the legislature assumes reality in the eyes of a constituent when he does something which touches that constituent personally."[1] And because this is so, a legislator is given little room to strive for greatness, to look at the larger picture, or to apply broad general principles to the major issues of the day. Most constituents do not expect their legislators to be statesmen, or geniuses, or authorities on the law. They do expect them to care for the little, individual problems that confront the citizen in his day-to-day living.

It is precisely because most legislative bills do not concern many people directly and because they do concern a few vitally that the legislative climate is what it is. It is this phenomenon that makes errand boys and special pleaders out of legislators. This situation is, in fact, an important consideration in the determination of the caliber of legislative personnel, in the tendency of interest groups to "go to Washington" on the most important issues, in the general lack of policy leadership to be found among legislators, and in the general status level of legislatures as social institutions.

This chapter will lay out the general structure, organization, powers, and behavior patterns of legislatures and legislators.

THE LEGISLATIVE FUNCTION

The modern function of the legislature in the governmental process, that of declaring and thus legitimatizing the law, is a relatively recent one in Western civilization. Traditionally, it belonged to the courts. The oldest functions of legislative bodies in our civilization are those of debate, criticism, and investigation.

DEVELOPMENT OF ASSEMBLIES To understand the trend in the use of legislative bodies as a part of the total process of policy making, it is necessary to place these institutions in their historical context. Representative assemblies developed in Europe in about the thirteenth century out of the feudal obligation of vassals to provide information and counsel to the sovereign. At first, these early assemblymen served chiefly to petition the king and to enter formal complaints against him and his bureaucracy. Later, especially in England, they developed the

[1] Richard L. Neuberger, "I Go to the Legislature," *Survey Graphic,* vol. 30, p. 373 ff., July, 1941.

right, on behalf of the influential classes, to give or withhold consent when the king proposed unusual expenditures or risky undertakings. Under the colonial-frontier influence, American legislative bodies, even before the War for Independence, began to develop a positive voice in decision making, although in most colonies the governor was very powerful. With the fall from favor of executives during that war, the new state legislatures became highly influential. The frontier influence of egalitarianism encouraged this trend and for much of the nineteenth century governors remained in eclipse as molders of policy. This same period was also the golden age of parliamentary power in the European democracies. Although they were powerful in policy making, early assemblies were, as a result of restricted suffrage along class lines, less representative than are American assemblies today.

With the rise of a complicated, technological society and with the increase in governmental functions that accompanied urbanization, policy leadership came to be expected of the executive. As a result, the popular assembly began to return to its historic function. But because Americans do not remember the popular assembly as basically a monitor, there has been much criticism of executive "usurpation" and of the "bureaucracy taking over." The essentially negative function of the legislature as a check upon the executive represents, then, more the reestablishment of the traditional pattern than the relegating of the legislature to a lesser role.

As this change in function has taken place, assembly leaders have expanded the exercise of the old power of investigation. Procedures by which the power of inquiry can be exercised in a responsible manner consistent with the liberty of individuals have not kept pace, however. The development of such procedures is a matter of prime importance to the legislatures of our time and its solution seems necessary for the preservation of effective democracy. The only democratic alternative, that of returning policy leadership to the assemblies, seems unrealistic. European history in the twentieth century is a continuous record of the failure of assemblies to develop procedures by which they might exercise a significant part in the process of government. The record is ominous, indicating the urgency attached to the need for working out a modern function for assemblies at all levels in the United States.

LEGISLATURES AND THE PURSE The central struggle between modern legislatures and executives has been one concerned with control over policies of raising and spending money, a struggle that began in the Middle Ages. As a logical and perhaps necessary part of the increasing power of the executive, a shift has occurred from legislative fiscal policy making to a growing emphasis upon the development of the executive budget, as was discussed in Chapter 3. As a result of the change, responsibility for innovation in the areas of taxation and appropriations is placed in the hands of the executive, with the legislative body serving to review them. This represents a return to traditional practice. A major job of the early assembly was to approve or disapprove proposed executive fiscal policies.

Nearly all states in the 1970s had some kind of executive budget, though in several the legislature was attempting to retain control of budget makeup, and in all it retained the final decision on appropriations. A few states have a budget board, with the governor as chairman and with other members drawn from either the legislative body, other elective administrative posts, or both. In North Carolina, it is customary for the appropriate legislative committee heads to work with the governor's budget officer throughout the process of assembling the budget. In Texas, two budget bureaus exist: one is headed by the governor's budget officer, the other is the Legislative Budget Board. The staff of each prepares a document for public and legislative consideration. In most of the states, however, the proposed budget is that proposed by the governor and his staff.

When legislatures were supreme, members of the tax and appropriation committees in each house made up the budget, working out differences among themselves on an informal basis. Today, these committees continue to operate, dissecting the executive budget, listening to interest-group representatives and agency personnel, bringing to bear their own often considerable interest and store of information, and helping to center the spotlight of publicity upon the process that determines the public's tax load. The policy-making initiative has been lost by the assemblies representing the public and nothing is more indicative of this than the trend toward the executive budget. But through its actions in reviewing the taxing and spending proposals of executives and administrators, in modifying them, and in sometimes withholding approval, the assemblies continue to perform an ancient function. In doing so, they contribute vitally to the maintenance of a democratic system of government.

STATE LEGISLATIVE STRUCTURE

SIZES OF LEGISLATIVE BODIES   There is no generally accepted basis for representation in American legislatures, and the size of each house seems to have depended originally upon considerations of expediency at the time the constitution was drafted; subsequent changes have depended upon similar factors whenever legislatures have been reapportioned. It is significant that a reapportionment is likely to result in an increase in the size of at least one house.

The membership in the upper houses of legislatures varies from 17 in Delaware and Nevada to 67 in Minnesota. The lower houses have an even greater range: from 35 in Delaware to 400 in New Hampshire. The enormous size of the lower houses in New England, relative to population, results from the fact that the town has been used there as the representative unit. New rules on reapportionment may force a change in this. Legislative houses tend to be quite small, commonly under 100 members, in the West.

TERMS OF OFFICE   The term of office for legislators seems to be just as haphazard as the size of legislative bodies. Generally, members of the upper house enjoy a longer term than their colleagues in the lower house. About two-thirds of the senates have four-year terms; the others, two years. The overwhelming majority of lower houses have two-year terms. The pattern varies greatly, however. In some legislatures, the four-year terms are staggered so that part of the membership comes up for election every two years.

PREREQUISITES AND PERQUISITES   As with governors, certain qualifications are usually required of legislators. They must be citizens, have resided in the state a certain length of time, have reached a certain age (senators usually have a higher minimum-age requirement than representatives), and be registered or eligible voters.

The pay for legislators has historically been small, and remains so in most states. The task of representing one's friends and neighbors was thought to be a civic duty. Seats were usually occupied, in pre-1850 America, either by well-to-do persons with a sense of social obligation (and a desire to protect their wealth) or by farmers who had a minimum of chores after harvest and before spring planting. However, social changes have since brought demands for better pay for legislators. Working-class representatives can ill afford to become legislators unless the salary is good or they are paid by a trade union while attending sessions. Merchants find it a sacrifice to leave their shops today, given present competitive conditions. The general emphasis upon getting ahead makes legislative service a liability rather than a business asset for all but a few types of persons, such as members of the legal profession. To many lawyers, especially younger ones, serving a few terms at the state capital is effective advertising. Similarly, some "organization men" are encouraged by their firms to seek legislative seats.

With the pressure for increased salaries has come a tendency to remove from state constitutions the severe restrictions on pay that once were common. Until recent years, legislators were frequently limited to $3 or $4 a day, and the number of days this could be drawn was also limited. The argument was often presented that these circumstances subjected legislators to undue influence by lobbyists who were happy to provide for meals and assume other expenses of the low-paid legislator, and in some states outright bribery was once fairly common. On the other hand, there is no convincing evidence that increased pay has improved the caliber of legislators, however one may measure such an obscure concept. It is certainly true, however, that overt bribery has declined, but whether this is the result of better pay or of changing social conditions remains unproved.

Salaries and allowances range from $5 a day in North Dakota and Rhode Island to $16,000 a year in California. In addition to base pay, legislators may get extra compensation for special sessions and are commonly given travel allowances. Additional allowances are commonly made for stationery, postage, telephone, and "expenses." In New York, expense allowances range from $3,000 to $4,500 per year.

In Texas, as an example of the cost of being a legislator, members receive a maximum of $3,000 for a regular session. It has been estimated that the typical member can just meet his expenses at this figure, assuming that the campaign that resulted in his being elected cost him nothing and that his business losses were zero. Neither assumption is, of course, often realistic.[2]

SESSIONS After the corn was picked, Christmas reverently observed, and the New Year boisterously brought in, the squires of nineteenth-century rural America took off for the state capital where they could, with reasonable convenience, remain until spring planting time. After that, however, they would stay with great reluctance. In those simpler days, legislative sessions were brief.

The length of sessions was constitutionally limited, commonly to 60 or 90 days, in some states during the last half of the nineteenth century in an effort to limit the activities of legislatures, which had fallen into disrepute. However, the demands of contemporary government are such that, in practice, the work of legislatures cannot usually be completed in so short a time. Several devices have been developed to circumvent the obsolete limitation. One is that of "covering the clock," thereby pretending that the legislators are not aware that the time limit has expired. In this fashion, it is possible to extend the session to an amount of time equal to that of the legal session plus the number of days the governor, who is not permitted by the courts to use this subterfuge, has to consider a bill before signing or vetoing it. Another device is to adjourn and go immediately into special session. In some states, the constitutions have been amended to extend the time limit or to do away with it.

Biennial sessions, common in the last century, met in odd-numbered years only, but this pattern is changing along with the general trend toward longer sessions. Several states have formally amended their constitutions to provide for annual sessions. In others, even in such relatively sparsely populated states as Wyoming, annual sessions are in fact the rule, because a special session is called for January of each even-numbered year. In some states, the governor alone can determine the subject matter that may be considered at a special session; in others, the rules of the legislature are controlling.

[2] *Compensation of Legislators and Frequency of Legislative Sessions,* Texas Legislative Council, 1956, chap. 3.

BICAMERALISM Several colonial legislatures consisted of one house, although most of them were bicameral. In the nineteenth century, however, the two-house system became universal in the United States, partly in imitation of the federal government, partly because it permitted the constituencies to be divided according to two different methods. It fitted nicely the politician's constant desire to strike a compromise. The chances are that representation under a two-house system will satisfy everyone to some degree, and this is more important politically than completely satisfying a few. The usual pattern was, and remains, one of basing one house largely on area (often using local government units as a rough measure), the other largely on population.

The fashion of the reform movement of several decades ago was to call for the adoption of unicameral legislatures. It was argued that the two-house system allows for "passing the buck," obscures responsibility for legislative decisions, encourages deadlocks, and offers an additional excuse for gerrymandering, since efforts will be made to find a basis other than population for representation in one house in order to help justify the existence of bicameralism.

Under the leadership of an outstanding reformer, Sen. George Norris, Nebraska adopted unicameralism, and the plan went into effect in 1937. It appears to have worked satisfactorily, but there has been relatively little interest in it elsewhere, though it is still strongly supported by some reformers. The requirement of having each house based only on population, imposed by the United States Supreme Court in 1964, caused some reformers to wonder if two houses any longer could be justified. However, even if members of the two houses were elected from identical districts with identical terms (which is not usually the case), differences in tenure, personality, and other relevant factors would still exist.

Many cities once had bicameral councils, but this pattern has now been almost completely abandoned at the municipal level. Reformers objected to bicameralism in cities, considering it a device for obscuring responsibility and for encouraging a parochial "errand-boy" approach to representation by councilmen.

Good government can probably be achieved within the bicameral system if the public and political leaders desire it. On the other hand, "buck passing," the obscuring of responsibility, and other alleged weaknesses in the system could easily be transferred to unicameralism by willful legislators. Reformers who look to structural change as a means for overcoming behavior patterns they find offensive give too little credit to the imaginativeness and creative ability of the American politician.

LEGISLATIVE ORGANIZATION AND PROCEDURE

State legislatures follow generally the organizational and procedural patterns of Congress. While there are some differences among the states as to detail, the basic pattern of decentralized policy making through the committee system is characteristic.

PRESIDING OFFICERS In the lower house, the speaker presides. He is, in form, elected by the entire membership. In practice, the choice is normally made in a caucus of members of the majority party or faction. Sometimes the actual selection is made by a relatively few top leaders. The vote on the speakership is commonly a mere formality, but it is usually the one test of party or factional loyalty that must not be failed. A legislator may defect on an important roll call later in the session without losing status as a party member. But if he does not support his group's candidate for speaker, he will not get majority party assignments to committees and will probably not be invited to caucuses. In this sense, it is the key vote of the session.

The speaker may be a powerful member in his own right, or may simply serve as a satrap for the leadership group. In states having a lieutenant governor, that official usually presides over the senate. Since he is not a member of the body, he does not have a vote except sometimes in case of a tie. Furthermore, he usually has very little influence over policy formulation, and this is true whether or not he is a member of the same party as the majority in the senate. While the speaker of the lower house appoints the standing committees in most states, this power less often goes to the lieutenant governor in the senate. Committees in the upper house are commonly named by a committee on committees which is normally made up of the most powerful members of the majority group in the senate.[3] When there is no lieutenant governor, the senate chooses its own presiding officer.

In many legislatures, two of the committees are often more important than the presiding officers. One is the committee on committees, mentioned above. The other is the rules committee. It is powerful, not because the permanent rules of a legislative body are changed very often, but because it is this group that can grant to a bill a special order or special rule, thus giving it a privileged position on the calendar of the house. In the rush of bills toward the end of the session, sometimes the only way a bill can get before the house is through such a special order from the rules committee. Hence this group may in practice be able to decide what is to be permitted to become law, a question that in theory belongs to the house as a whole. In some states it is traditional to permit only members of the majority party or faction to sit on the rules committee, thus keeping the tactical plans of the inner circle a secret.

OTHER OFFICERS AND EMPLOYEES The various sergeants at arms, clerks, secretaries, and typists who make up the work force of the legislature hold posts that usually represent important patronage for the membership. The majority party or faction parcels these out, often on a roughly geographical basis, with some perhaps going to the minority.

THE COMMITTEE SYSTEM Because state legislative houses, like Congress, are normally made up of a large number of persons and because the floor of such houses is not the most effective place for serious decision making or for political horse trading, American legislatures traditionally do most of their work through committees. The committee system seems to be necessary where the deliberative body is large, but the approach used in state legislatures has been widely criticized because the system obscures the nature of the work of the legislature, confuses responsibility to the public, and frequently allows

---

[3] Details on legislative membership and organization may be found in the most recent volume of the *Book of the States,* Council of State Governments, Chicago, and in the volumes of the American Commonwealth Series, each of which describes a single state.

a minority of the house (the committee majority) to determine policy. Standing committees, as in city and county governments when they are used, tend to take over administrative functions or at least to become definitely involved in them.

Committees in legislatures operate in basically the same manner as do those in Congress or in local governing bodies that use them (many small governing boards and councils do not). The legislative house as a whole becomes chiefly a ratifying body for the actions of the committees. The house can override a committee recommendation or relieve a committee of further consideration of a bill, but these things are not likely to happen, since each legislator—like each congressman—will tacitly agree to allow other legislators to be supreme in their committee areas if they will extend the same privilege to him. The committee is the key group in the legislative system.

There are some real advantages in the committee system. Legislative bodies, to provide adequately for representativeness, must be fairly large. If they are to get their work done, the committee system is a logical means by which to expedite the job. Members of committees often become specialists in their fields, knowing much more about a specific subject than the average legislator. They may learn enough to make knowledgeable recommendations to their colleagues concerning programs and budgets.

The committee system provides a means of specialization of effort within the legislature. Similar policies of specialization are followed in the executive and judicial branches. In our complicated contemporary world, we should have to attract into the legislature persons of an extremely high level of training and intelligence to serve as *general* overseers of those who carry out policy in all of its technical and otherwise complex ramifications. The committee system allows legislators to concentrate on a smaller universe of administrative activities and makes it easier for them to carry on one of the most vital democratic functions, that of criticism and review.

Although it is not observed as rigidly in most legislatures as it is in Congress, the seniority system of assigning committee seats is often important. In states where the vote on the speakership of the lower house is not rigidly along party lines, but is subject to negotiation or "deals," a choice assignment may be promised in return for a badly needed vote, and this consideration may outweigh that of seniority.

Perhaps seniority is also somewhat less observed because until recent decades legislative turnover was very high and it was not easy to rank members by years of service. But the idea of "wait your turn" is important in many of our social institutions, beginning with the children's play group, and it is not unnatural for ranking members to want, and to be permitted to receive, the most powerful or desirable assignments. Committee chairmanships are often assigned exclusively on the basis of seniority within the majority party, and it is frequently almost impossible to remove an incompetent from such a position if he outranks other party members in years of service.

There are usually many committees in each house, though they range from less than 10 to more than 60 in various legislatures around the country. Exceptions to the general pattern are to be found in Connecticut, Maine, and Massachusetts, which depend wholly or partly upon joint committees, with membership from both houses sitting together. Although reform efforts in recent decades have aimed at reducing the number of committees so as to encourage more concentration on important bills, legislators like the prestige of serving on many committees and of a chairmanship. A large number of committees is also convenient because it provides handy places into which to shunt new members as well as potentially influential members of the minority party or faction. Thus, committees were once so specialized in the Minnesota House of Representatives that there was a committee on binding twine and another on (railroad) sleeping cars.

PARTY ORGANIZATION AND DISCIPLINE No thorough study of the function of the political party in state legislatures has been made, but it varies a great deal. An effective, well-financed lobbyist could rather easily achieve considerable power in California with its weak party system, but would find this much more difficult in New York where party discipline in the legislature has been strong for decades. In New York, the political party itself to a large extent finances legislative campaigns; in California, the candidate gets much of his support from interest-group representatives. The groups also pay directly into the party treasuries and hope thus to be influential, but their impact is likely to be weaker through this approach.

In Vermont, legislation results from the balancing off of interest-group demands before the legislature itself, with the parties of almost no importance in relation to policy positions. There is no party line because, as in the Southern states and in some others elsewhere, nearly all the legislators are of the same party.[4] This is in contrast to Connecticut, a state with a two-party system. Stands on issues there tend to be divided along urban-rural or urban-suburban lines. Since most of the Democrats are from urban areas, and the Republicans from suburban and rural areas, a party cleavage is produced on many issues.[5] Under these circumstances, party control is meaningful, and uncooperative members are sometimes disciplined; their pet bills may be buried, or they may even be denied renomination.

This pattern of control is probably not to be found in many legislatures. In states with the one-party system, party caucuses would be meaningless and the quasi nonpartisanship of the legislature in such states results in turn in encouraging parties to break up into factions. In states with strong two-party systems, much of the voting is along party lines, and the amount of this appears to be significantly higher in those two-party states which are larger and more urban. In the large, two-party industrial states, a high level of party voting in the legislature is to some extent habitual and party alignments largely follow national politics.[6]

In such states, however, each party tends to move toward a moderate position, and representatives from districts that are atypical of the party not infrequently show independence of party discipline. Furthermore, a great many legislative roll calls are unanimous, and the number of cases of clear alignment of one party against another are relatively few.

LEGISLATIVE PROCEDURE   The pattern of introduction, hearings, floor debate, and rules on passage vary somewhat from state to state, but in general it follows that used in Congress. The accompanying figure outlines the passage of a bill according to the rules in Kansas. Bills

[4] See Oliver Garceau and Corinne Silverman, "A Pressure Group and the Pressured," *American Political Science Review,* vol. 48, pp. 672–691, September, 1954.

[5] W. Duane Lockard, "Legislative Politics in Connecticut," *American Political Science Review,* vol. 48, pp. 166–173, March, 1954.

[6] Malcolm E. Jewell, *The State Legislature: Politics and Practice,* Random House, Inc., New York, 1962.

may be drafted by the attorney general's office at the request of some state agency or of the governor; they may be written by a member, by a lobbyist, or by an attorney for an interest group; or they may be drawn up, in some states, by the legislative bill-drafting service at the request of a member.

The key to the fate of a bill often rests with the committee to which it is assigned. The presiding officer or the committee that has the power to decide which committee should receive the bill often determines the fate of the measure. One committee chairman may view the bill with definite favor; another may be determined to kill it and may be influential enough to do so even though he knows that the bill would pass if it reached the floor of the house.

Procedures as to public hearings vary from state to state and according to the assumed importance of a bill. In some states, the capitol has few rooms adequate for public hearings. Sometimes tradition does not support the demand for public hearings and few are held, even on matters of great moment. Or hearings may be held on a bill if the sponsors demand it and are influential. The hearings offer an opportunity for lobbyists to make formal statements and for individual legislators to question witnesses. Legislators sometimes use the hearings as a sounding board in an attempt to learn the extent of support a bill enjoys. They may also use them as a means of giving favorable or unfavorable publicity to a bill.

If bills pass the two houses in even very slightly different form, they must go to a conference committee which is usually made up of equal representation from the two houses; however the presiding officer or committee that has the power to decide who is to sit on the conference committee again is often in a position to expedite or to impede the passage of the bill. It is easy to stack the conference committee with friends or enemies of the bill. In some states, however, it is customary for the originating house to accept the amendments of the second house without holding a conference.

Once a bill is passed, there is commonly some kind of waiting period before it goes into effect. For example, in New Mexico, laws go into effect 90 days after the adjournment of the legislature, except general appropriation bills which go into effect as soon as approved by the governor or when passed over his veto. Any act "necessary for the preservation of the public peace, health or safety" also takes

THE HOUSE OF REPRESENTATIVES IN FORMAL SESSION

THE SENATE

ADMINISTRATIVE OFFICIALS

Introducing member	Staff of the Chief Clerk of the House			Speaker of the House	House Standing Committee	Committee of the Whole House	The Senate	Secretary of the Senate	President of the Senate	State Printer	Secretary of State	Governor
	Chief Clerk	Reading Clerk	Other Clerks									
Introduction of bill		First reading	Record of first reading							Printing of bill		
		Second reading	Record of second reading	Reference to Standing Committee	Consideration by Standing Committee							
			Reading of report of Standing Committee	Record of report of Standing Committee								
			Reading of report of Committee of the Whole	Record of report of Committee of the Whole	Consideration by Committee of the Whole							
			Third reading Roll call and vote	Record of third reading and vote			Procedure similar to that in House	Certification				
Certification			Reading of message from Senate									
			Record of bill's return from Senate									
	Signature of Chief Clerk of House			Signature of Speaker of the House				Signature of Secretary of State	Signature of President of Senate	Printing of bill on parchment	Preparation of correct copy for enrollment	
												Signature of Governor

The odyssey of a bill. This one originated in the Kansas House of Representatives. (Source: Rhoten A. Smith, *The Life of a Bill*, rev. ed., Governmental Research Center, the University of Kansas, Lawrence, 1961, pp. 16–17.)

immediate effect providing that two-thirds of the members of each house agree to it.

In a sense, a new law must go through a still further process of refinement before it becomes binding as a part of the rules that control the actions of people. The legislature could not be specific enough in its language, even if it tried, to make the meaning of every part of the law completely clear. A new act must, therefore, often be "interpreted" by rulings of the attorney general which have the force and effect of law unless overruled by the courts. Important laws, especially if they venture into new areas of governmental activity or prescribe new procedures are often tested finally in the supreme court of the state before their full meaning is clarified. Once in a while, a state law will even go to the United States Supreme Court for interpretation if it seems to conflict with a federal law or the United States Constitution.

LEGISLATIVE POWERS

In addition to its powers of lawmaking, the state legislature has ceremonial, constituent, executive, administrative, and judicial functions.

CEREMONIAL FUNCTIONS   Although the legislative body acting collectively, or the members individually, are not called upon so often as is the governor to perform ritualistic functions, they do spend much of their time on this sort of thing. Boy Scout troop leaders in the balcony are introduced. A state Olympic swimmer is congratulated on a victory. As with the governor, such activity is often considered by the legislator as important to his political future.

CONSTITUENT FUNCTIONS   Legislatures have the power to submit proposals for constitutional amendment to the voters, as was discussed in Chapter 1. This, together with the power to submit the question of calling a constitutional convention, is known as the "constituent power" of the legislature.

EXECUTIVE POWERS   A great many appointments are made by governors to administrative positions, to boards and commissions, and, in some states, to judicial posts. These appointments are generally subject to approval by the senate. That body, in granting its approval, is exercising an executive function that stems from the days when the upper house in some of the colonial legislatures served as the executive council, advising the governor. In a few states in New England and in the South, the legislature elects some of the judges as well as some of the administrative officers. Legislatures also commonly prescribe detailed organizational structure for each state agency and may also spell out quite specifically the administrative procedures that they are to follow in performing their functions.

The power to investigate is a traditional legislative function. Legislatures generally have extensive powers in this field, although they do not ordinarily use them to the extent that Congress does. Investigations may deal with suspected corruption, mismanagement, or "inefficiency" in an agency. If the governor or other elected official is not of the same party or faction as the majority in one house, an election year usually produces a rash of investigations of the administration. Sometimes these fishing expeditions find cases of improper behavior; at other times they only appear to do so. In either case, the material is generally useful against the party in power or the particular candidate for office.

Quite a few committee investigations are aimed at exploring areas where new legislation may be needed. In the short, hectic sessions that are characteristic of most legislatures, there is little opportunity for careful study or extensive hearings. Between-sessions investigations help to overcome this deficiency. In addition, the legislative investigation is often an important device to expose and to safeguard against executive actions that are corrupt, inefficient, autocratic, or unresponsive to society's values and wants.

JUDICIAL POWERS As in the case of Congress, legislatures are the judges of the qualifications of their own members. Usually, they can determine whether or not they will seat a member whose claim by right of election is clouded for some reason. They can also sit in judgment of a member who is accused of wrongdoing and may expel him. The impeachment powers possessed by legislatures are also judicial in nature. None of these is often employed, however.

LEGISLATIVE STAFF ASSISTANCE

Legislators in quite a few states, in an attempt to improve the quality of their work and to relieve themselves of their dependence upon lobbyists and the administrative bureaucracy, have employed professional staffs to assist them. In many states, however, they have not done this, even though the cost would be relatively small. It is likely that many legislators do not understand the nature of staff work or the advantages it can produce.

Legislative assistance is usually centered, if it exists, in a legislative reference bureau, or a bill-drafting service. Many states have legislative councils consisting of selected legislators, sometimes aided by a research staff. This group works between sessions, investigating or drawing up legislation and perhaps preparing programs and making recommendations for their colleagues' consideration at the next session. Generally these councils have greatly influenced legislation. But legislators who are not named to the council are sometimes jealous of its status and power. They may resent the fact that it sometimes presents to them at the beginning of a session a completely prepared policy proposal, with council members primed with answers to questions the nonmembers have not yet even had a chance to formulate.

LOBBYING

The old-style professional lobbyist, working simultaneously for several interest groups and carrying a black bag filled with temptation, is passing from the political scene. Today, the most effective lobbyists are generally officers of influential organized groups, respected citizens, careful of their facts and persons whose sense of ethics is in accord with the society in which they live.

The functions of the lobby and its method of operation are essentially the same before both state legislatures and Congress; these are discussed in two other publications of this series.[7]

---

[7] Joseph P. Harris, *Congress and the Legislative Process,* 2d ed., McGraw-Hill Book Company, New York, 1971; and Hugh Bone and Austin Ranney, *Politics and Voters,* 3d ed., McGraw-Hill Book Company, New York, 1971.

THE ISSUE OF APPORTIONMENT

The number of seats in each house of the legislature is usually determined by the constitution or by constitutional formula, although this is not always the case. It is traditional in America to divide constituencies into single-member districts. There are, however, many instances of multimember districts and of the election of some members at large. The creation of these districts and the assignment of seats to them is called "apportionment" and it is over reapportionment of the legislature that a great many political battles have been fought and will be fought in the future.

Rapid urbanization has produced great shifts in population. It has been necessary to revise legislative districts after each census in order to have equal numbers of persons in them. But it has been common in the twentieth century for state legislatures to fail to make the necessary district changes.

REAPPORTIONMENT AS A JUDICIAL QUESTION Although in the early 1970s the issue of apportionment appears to be quite settled, individual conflicts will occur each time a legislature, apportionment commission, or court acts on redistricting. Even though "one man, one vote" is now established, it is worth reviewing how it became public policy. In 1926, an effort was made to require the Illinois Supreme Court to order the Illinois legislature to reapportion itself in compliance with the state constitution. The court refused to act, claiming that under the separation-of-powers doctrine it had no right to order the legislature to do anything.[8] The ruling in this case was widely supported in the judiciary and advocates of legislative reapportionment were forced to concentrate their pressures on generally unwilling legislators. The picture remained unchanged until well after World War II.

The *Magraw* case of 1958 was a landmark decision, even though it did not reach the United States Supreme Court.[9] It was significant in that a federal district court judge accepted jurisdiction in a case involv-

---

[8] *Fergus v. Marks,* 321 Ill. 510 (1926).

[9] *Magraw v. Donovan,* 163 F. Supp. 1589 (1958); dismissed after the legislature was reapportioned, 177 F. Supp. 803 (1959).

ing the apportionment of a state legislature. Previously, state and federal courts avoided the question either by arguing that the separation-of-powers doctrine prevented the courts from imposing their will upon the legislature, or by arguing as in the *Colegrove* case,[10] that the apportionment of a legislature was a "political question" for which there were no judicial guidelines and hence no justiciable controversy.

The next major case was *Baker v. Carr*,[11] in 1962. In this case the United States Supreme Court for the first time accepted jurisdiction in a reapportionment case. The court then went on to rule that the lower federal court could consider whether the Tennessee legislature had violated the equal-protection-of-the-laws clause of the Fourteenth Amendment by failing to reapportion itself as required by the Constitution.

The *Baker* case was significant because the Court had accepted jurisdiction in apportionment cases and because it had ruled that failure to apportion could deprive a citizen of his constitutional right to equal protection of the laws. Beyond this, all it did was to remand the case with instructions that the lower court take jurisdiction and consider the questions raised by the plaintiff. The direction in which the Court would move had been indicated, however. The next year, 1963, it ruled that the Georgia county-unit system of voting in primary elections for the governorship and for congressmen, a system under which the person who carried a majority of counties would win even with fewer total votes than his opponent, also deprived citizens of their right to equal protection.[12] This case made it clear that by equal protection the court meant equality in terms of total population or total potential votes, in other words, "one man, one vote."

The next year, the Court went the full distance to the logical conclusion. In February, it ruled that when legislatures determine the boundaries of congressional districts they must make sure "as nearly as practical, one man's vote in a Congressional election must be worth as much as another's."[13] And in June, 1964, in the *Reynolds*

[10] *Colegrove v. Green,* 328 U.S. 549 (1946).
[11] *Baker v. Carr,* 369 U.S. 186 (1962).
[12] *Gray v. Sanders,* 371 U.S. 821 (1963).
[13] *Westberry v. Sanders,* 376 U.S. 1 (1964).

case, the court ruled that both houses of a state legislature must be apportioned as strictly as possible according to population.[14] The Court did not indicate how much of a margin of variation it would permit, but it held again that the equal protection clause applied to apportionment. In this historic case, the Court also dealt with two touchy arguments, arguments upon which the opponents of straight population representation had based their hopes. It held that the pattern of representation in the United States Congress, in which no state can be deprived of its equal representation in the Senate without its own permission, did not apply. The Court specifically pointed out that the Senate apportionment was the result, not of the estimate by the founding fathers of what was equitable, but of a political deal necessary in order for the United States Constitution to be politically acceptable to the less populous states. The Court also ruled that popular votes relative to apportionment were not relevant to the case, that is, that one's civil rights cannot be voted away by popular majority. The majority opinion, written by Chief Justice Earl Warren, said that, "a citizen's constitutional rights can hardly be infringed upon because a majority of the people choose to do so."

The *Reynolds* case actually involved six cases. One justice dissented from the entire decision and two others dissented in part. The sweeping decision promptly produced a wave of proposals to set it aside. A number of bills and resolutions were introduced in Congress. The one receiving the most support was that by Senator Everett Dirksen of Illinois, who proposed a constitutional amendment which would permit the states to have one house based on something other than straight population. Many state legislatures—still unapportioned—petitioned Congress either to submit a constitutional amendment similar to the Dirksen proposal, or to have Congress call a national constitutional convention, at which such a proposal could be considered. In 1965 and 1966, the Dirksen proposal narrowly missed securing the two-thirds vote needed in the United States Senate and the issue of reapportionment remained very much conflict ridden. In the meanwhile, both state and federal courts issued rulings pressuring states to comply with the *Reynolds* decision.

[14] *Reynolds v. Sims,* 377 U.S. 533 (1964).

Just how much variation from strict population apportionment the courts will allow was still unclear in 1971. Whether or not the Court's decision was fair to all segments of the population and in "the public interest" is an ideological question that cannot be answered by political scientists. The decision, however, is likely to stand as the basis upon which future state government will have to be built.

The potential effects of reapportionment are considerable. It could encourage the states to assume a major part of meeting the problems of an urban-industrial society by increasing the representation of core cities and, especially, suburban areas. Some studies indicate, however, that the wealth of a state is more important than is apportionment in determining expenditure levels. Even so, legislatures that reflect by number actual life styles of the population would seem more likely to seek to meet the problems of concern to the greatest number of people than would those that do not.

THOSE WHO SERVE

About two-thirds of all legislators are businessmen, lawyers, and farmers. The membership of the last group has never been so great as folklore would have it—rural areas have always been represented largely by small-town merchants and lawyers. Very few skilled craftsmen or hourly rated employees of any kind are members. Since the beginning of the present century, the occupational patterns of legislators appear to have changed little; however, the average age of incumbents has increased somewhat, there has been a steady increase in the average amount of education, and the average amount of legislative experience each session has been increasing, although legislative turnover remains high. There are far fewer venal members today, and far fewer who will accept direct bribes or operate shakedown rackets by threatening to pass harassing legislation. In all of these trends, the legislator reflects similar developments in the nation and its economy generally.

One cannot be optimistic about an upturn in the value of legislative stock. The long-time unrepresentative character of legislative bodies encouraged urbanites to turn to their city councils or to Congress for assistance in meeting the social needs that have arisen in contemporary urban America. They have also turned to the governor as their hope for policy leadership that reflects consideration of the kinds of problems they deem important.

The President's Commission on Intergovernmental Relations noted:

> In power and influence [state legislatures] are no longer as dominant as they were, partly because of the ascendancy of the National Government, partly because of the increased influence of the State executive, but primarily because they had not found effective solutions to problems that become more chronic and more difficult to cope with in a rapidly changing society.[15]

Whether the low esteem in which state legislatures are generally held can be replaced by a status position more in keeping with the important function of that institution is problematical. The answer probably rests largely with the contemporary legislative leaders. It is they who are faced with a dilemma: the acceptance of low status or the acceptance of the important but expensive demands placed upon government by today's urbanites.

THE LEGISLATOR BESIEGED

The greatest dilemma confronting legislators today lies in a conflict between the need for information and the inability or unwillingness to trust those who possess it. The legislator is a generalist making policy in an age of specialization. With some exceptions, he is an amateur whose best skill is that of reflecting the values and wants of his constituents—values and wants that may be regarded by the experts in particular fields of governmental activity as obstacles to what is regarded in their professional fields as sound policy.

The legislator may wish to be a wise policy maker, but he feels that both the expert lobbyists of various interest groups and the spokesmen for the state's increasingly skilled bureaucracy are untrustworthy. He sees them as people trying to sell him a "bill of goods." Are they asking for the ultimate? Or are they being reasonable? Is their "bedrock minimum" really a minimum, given the expectations of most citizens? Is the expert, be he a lobbyist or a bureaucrat, properly respect-

---

[15] *A Report to the President,* 1955, p. 38.

ful and understanding of the legislator's difficult task? Is his "expertise" forthrightly presented as a reflection of professional conviction, or is it designed merely to support a particular program or to whitewash administrative errors? The legislator wishes he knew.

The legislator fears that everyone is asking for the moon on a platter, hoping to get at least the platter. But he cannot be sure. How can he tell? Whom can he trust? He does not know. He is so disenchanted with "experts" that he does not even feel sure that the legislature should hire its own to give loyal opinions on what other experts say. Yet all of society is expecting him to take effective action to meet the demands of citizens. His job is a difficult one.

REVIEW QUESTIONS

1. Why are legislators not generally concerned with the "big" issues?

2. How does the contemporary function of the state legislature compare with the traditional function of popular assemblies?

3. What is the responsibility of state legislatures in relation to control of the public purse?

4. How have legislative sessions changed through the years? What are the reasons for the changes?

5. Explain the reasons for the predominance of bicameralism in state legislatures.

6. How does seniority in state legislatures compare with that in Congress?

7. What is the function of the political party in relation to the activities of state legislatures?

8. Describe the process by which a bill becomes law or dies in your state legislature.

9. Using news reports, give examples of the ceremonial, constituent, executive, and judicial functions of your state legislature.

10. Why have legislators generally been reluctant to hire professional staff?

11. Describe the apportionment pattern of your state legislature. What are the current issues concerning reapportionment in your state?

5 STATE AND LOCAL COURTS

In primitive societies, personal revenge for wrongs against one's family or kinsmen is the common approach, and most simple societies leave settlements to negotiations between families or clans.[1] But whatever the arrangement, it is imperative that every society, for the sake of its own stability, have a means for settling disputes and challenges to the established order—one that does not seriously disrupt the smooth operation of society.

As governments grow more complicated, man's social and econom-

[1] See E. Adamson Hoebel, *Anthropology: The Study of Man,* 3d ed., McGraw-Hill Book Company, New York, 1966, chap. 30.

ic horizons expand beyond the blood group. He begins to think in terms of the community and then of still larger social organizations. As social relationships become less personal and ways of earning a living more complicated, the law becomes more complex, and so do the legal codes and the institutions for administering them—the courts.

Crime, justice, equity, and other such terms are all cultural concepts. Their meaning comes out of the culture and is not the same in every nation, or even in every state or community within the United States. The notion of what is a fair settlement in a business disagreement, or the conditions under which a crime may be overlooked by the prosecutor or may result in a "not guilty" verdict even though the alleged act was obviously committed, are determined by the values of society. Similarly, judicial organization and administration reflect the values of society, and apply both criminal and civil law in accord with the dominant beliefs and interests in the community.

Once again, therefore, we should note that the institutions of government provide for decision making about the allocation of the prizes and deprivations of society. In the judicial process, the values of life, liberty, and property are assigned in a most direct fashion as far as the individual is concerned. In this arena, the typical citizen commonly comes in contact with his government from time to time during his life span and the awards and punishments of society's dominant values are his to experience. They may involve a minor cost (a $5 parking fine), be gratifying (a large cash settlement in a lawsuit), or represent the ultimate penalty (a death sentence).

JUSTICE AND THE CULTURE

In Texas in 1958, a striptease dancer convicted of possessing marijuana was sentenced to 15 years in prison, even though the search warrant at the time of her arrest did not state the reason for the search, and there was no evidence that she had attempted to use or sell the drug. At about the same time, an airline stewardess was given a suspended sentence on a similar charge, and a man convicted on six counts of transporting and selling heroin—a far more insidious narcotic than marijuana—was given a five-year sentence. Because of her occupation, the dancer had been resented by some women of her community. As one observer said: "That girl was framed like a window in a church, because she was endangerin' the morality of our fair city."[2]

THE CONCEPT OF JUSTICE   Justice is a relative concept and its administration is relative to time, place, and circumstance. In the individual case it depends upon the ideology, attitude, diligence, interest, and other considerations of the police officer, the prosecutor, the judge, the jurors, the defense attorney, the probation officer, and every other person who comes in contact with the case. It also makes a difference who you are. A police officer may take a different view toward a man in greasy overalls who stumbles out of a working-class tavern from what he will toward a man dressed in a well-tailored suit who stumbles out of the bar of an expensive hotel. The former may spend the night in the "drunk tank"; the latter may be helped to his room.

Differential justice of this type should not be confused, however, with the tendency of a jury to apply cultural values or the popular sentiment of the moment to a particular case. A jury will often refuse to convict a woman who kills her unfaithful husband, for example. In the South, the mores may prevent a jury from finding a white man guilty of a crime against a Negro. If the jurors believe the penalty is too severe for a particular crime, they will not convict regardless of the evidence, with the result that sometimes the legislature must modify the law to suit the jurors' concept of justice.

The judicial process as it exists in practice is often criticized, yet the people who make unfavorable comments may well be the same ones who dodge jury duty (it is easy to do so) or refuse to testify even though they suspect their testimony is needed by the plaintiff or the prosecutor. Certainly both of these acts are common on the part of Americans.

Great delays often occur before cases, either criminal or civil, come to trial, especially in more densely populated areas. "Justice delayed is justice denied," is a cliché, but it is often true. Witnesses die or disappear, the jury discounts an old wrong more than a recent wrong; evidence cannot be kept intact.

[2] Cases and quotation from John Bainbridge, *The Super-Americans,* Doubleday & Company, Inc., Garden City, N.Y., 1963.

Justice is also costly. Some efforts are being made to overcome this problem. The office of the public defender is becoming a more common institution to assist the person accused of a crime. Legal aid bureaus have become common in cities as a source of information in some kinds of cases, at least for the low-income person. These bureaus are run by incorporated charities, bar associations, social agencies, and other organizations. Yet even the middle-income person finds legal procedures a heavy financial burden, and the law, which grows ever more complicated, is totally unfathomable by the layman.

The number of lawsuits is decreasing, despite our population growth and the increasing complexity of our society. Appeals to higher courts are expensive, and few appeals are therefore taken, although failure to carry the case above the decisions of an incompetent or indolent trial judge may well result in the denial of justice. In contrast, the large corporation can afford to keep a case in court for years on appeals, not only to win a particular case, but to discourage other actions against the company. (The large corporation has its own cross to bear: juries tend to award generous judgments against it and sometimes to regard the person who defrauds it as something of a hero.) The wealthy person or corporation that hires a former state supreme court justice to argue its appeal before the supreme court or an incumbent legislator to argue its case before an administrative tribunal such as the liquor-control commission has an advantage over a less well-to-do opponent or the prosecutor in a criminal case.

The law is slow to change, and many of its rules, particularly those of evidence, are such as to permit injustice unnecessarily. The legal concept of insanity, for example, differs widely from the scientific knowledge gained from a study of psychosis. The courts may refuse to admit evidence which, to the layman, seems to be highly relevant—sometimes because the new knowledge has come too recently to be recognized.

American courts have always had something of the circus about them, and they hold a hypnotic attraction for people who find murder or rape trials an exciting and welcome change from their own dull lives. This pattern may be changing, and some courts are dignified today. Certainly the United States district courts fit this category, and their enormously prestigeful judges will ordinarily not permit the court to become too much of a theater. But judges are sometimes careless about the appearance of the courtroom, they may hesitate to clear it of spectators during spicy testimony lest they be reversed on appeal (one's civil rights guarantee a public trial), and newspapers attract crowds to the more spectacular trials as a result of their financial interest in dramatizing them. The theatrical setting in such cases probably does not contribute to a disinterested review of the evidence by either the judge or the jury. And of course, the fox-and-hounds nature of criminal trials will probably always keep them something of a show.

TRENDS IN JUDICIAL ADMINISTRATION Serious efforts are being made by bar associations, legislatures, judges, social service agencies, and others to keep the quality and character of judicial administration up to date. Changes have taken place; others are on the way. Thus, today:

> Courts rely less and less upon the participation of grand and petit juries ... the gap thus created has been more than filled by the infiltration of many kinds of experts. Administrative experts have supplanted the courts in many functional areas ... expert witnesses speak authoritatively on subjects which are too specialized for judges (or juries) to comprehend; the judges themselves become specialists in presiding over a relatively narrow class of cases, as in many functionally organized metropolitan courts; administrative assistants are assigned to help shoulder the labor of justices of state supreme courts. Sociologists and psychologists have increasingly taken over responsibility and authority to make decisions that used to be made by judges in such fields as juvenile delinquency and probation. ... The upshot of this is that the courts ... are becoming bureaucratized.[3]

Law and the judicial process, then, are parts of the total culture in which they exist and are subjected to the same kinds of pressures that affect our other institutions. In a day when most of our socially useful activities are dominated by the expert and the pattern of specialization, our courts are also coming to be dominated by the expert and to conform to the pattern of specialization.

[3] Glendon A. Schubert, Jr., "The Theory of 'The Public Interest' in Judicial Decision-making," *Midwest Journal of Political Science,* vol. 2, p. 24, February, 1958. Used by permission. See also his *The Public Interest,* The Free Press, New York, 1960, pp. 196–197.

ORGANIZATION OF STATE COURTS

Because of our federal system, federal courts and state courts have simultaneous jurisdiction over the same territory, people, and corporations. Despite this, the ordinary citizen is likely to have contact only with the latter, for the great bulk of domestic law, both criminal and civil, is based upon state statutory or common law or upon local ordinances. Cases that result are normally tried in state courts. There is a federal criminal law, but the typical criminal is far more likely to be tried in a state than in a federal court, although he is sometimes tried in each for the same offense for this is not legally considered to be double jeopardy.

GENERAL TRIAL COURTS The courts for hearing civil and criminal cases "in the first instance" are the backbone of the American judicial system. Most cases that the typical citizen is concerned with will come up before them. The quality of justice the individual receives and his image of the court system will depend largely upon the way in which these courts are administered. In most states, they are known as county courts, district courts, or circuit courts, although other names are also used and the nomenclature may not be uniform within a state. The larger cities, in particular, are likely to have their own court systems, parallel to, but independent of, the rest of the state courts and often using a different nomenclature.

In these courts, the criminal cases presented by the prosecutor or grand jury are tried (often before a jury) for the first time, as are all but the most minor civil actions (except cases involving the probating of wills). Appeals taken from the minor courts to the general trial courts are also really heard "in the first instance," since they are started over again from the beginning (tried *de novo,* the lawyers say).

Permanent records are kept of the proceedings of these courts, and they are therefore sometimes referred to as "courts of record." Except in unusual circumstances, one judge presides over the courtroom (several judges may serve a single district if it is populous enough). In most cases, the decision of the trial court is final. Although in theory appeal can almost always be taken to a higher court, in practice this is done only in unusual circumstances as for example, in civil cases where a great amount of money is involved or a well-to-do person or corporation wishes to test the constitutionality or learn the judicial meaning of a law, or in criminal cases where the defendant is well-to-do, or a defense fund has been collected for him, or his case has become a test case and is being financed by some group interested in civil liberties, such as the American Civil Liberties Union. Most litigants and criminal defendants must accept the findings of the trial court.

COURTS OF APPEAL   The most populous states usually have a court of appeals above the trial courts and below the state supreme court. These courts do not hear cases over from the beginning but rather receive written and oral arguments concerning points of law that were made a matter of dispute at the trial. Questions of fact are ordinarily not reviewed by appellate courts. Since law and not fact is being considered, there is no jury in appeal courts, and a multiple bench of from three to nine judges is used.

The intermediate courts sometimes are organized separately for criminal and civil appeals; they may be set up on the basis of appellate judicial districts, or there may be only one such court for the entire state. Titles vary, but they are usually known by such names as the "court of appeals" or the "superior court." Under customary procedure, decisions are reached by a majority vote of the judges who hear the case, and one of the judges writes a formal decision explaining the facts of the case briefly, setting out the legal reasoning used (or said to have been used) by the judges in reaching their decision and stating the ruling of the court and the disposal of the case. The latter will usually involve either sustaining the findings of the lower court or reversing them. In the latter case, the usual order is for a retrial in conformity with the findings of the decision.

In some states, the decision of the intermediate court is final unless a constitutional question is involved, in which case appeal can be taken to the state supreme court. This arrangement frees the highest court for intensive consideration of the most important cases. In some populous states no intermediate court of appeal has been established, however, with the result that the supreme court is the only appellate court and is therefore forced to consider cases in large numbers, hurriedly, and with a chronic backlog on the docket.

STATE SUPREME COURTS   The general function of the state supreme court (in New York, Kentucky, and Maryland, called the "court of appeals") was indicated above. Like other appeals courts, it consists of from three to nine judges and generally follows the same procedure. The principal difference is found in the fact that the supreme courts are the courts of final decision from which there is no judicial appeal on any ground except for those rare instances where a case within state jurisdiction can be argued to involve a federal question or the state court procedure to violate the United States Constitution. In these unusual circumstances, it is possible to appeal from the state supreme court to the United States Supreme Court. Such cases are heard by the highest court in the land only at its own discretion, and it accepts only cases involving basic questions.

In a few instances, a state supreme court hears cases in original jurisdiction—the case is tried initially before the court—but this is uncommon. In some cases it offers advisory opinions at the request of the governor, some other state official, a legislative house, or a legislator, but in most states this function is reserved for the attorney general, and the court hears only those cases in which a real issue at law in a specific case is involved.

All courts, but especially courts of final jurisdiction, have great public policy-making powers. They must give the fine edge of meaning to legislative acts and administrative orders since they apply these general policies to specific cases. They also decide the meaning of the state constitution and apply it to cases. Although decisions are stated in the ritualistic language of the law, the court in such cases is actually serving as a political body; that is, it is making policy that has the force and effect of law.

Throughout our history, conflict, tension, and competition have existed between state supreme courts and the only judicial agency that may review their decisions, the United States Supreme Court. The latter restricts its own jurisdiction quite severely. It accepts state court interpretations of state law and state constitutions except where it considers them to be in conflict with federal law or the United States Constitution. In 1959, out of the tens of thousands of cases disposed of by the 50 state high courts, the Supreme Court in Washington reviewed only 30. It rejected 93 percent of the requests it received. But it is probably more significant that over one-fourth of the cases decided during that term were brought up from the state courts (30 out of 105).[4]

[4] See William J. Brennan, Jr., "State Court Decisions and the Supreme Court," in Alan F. Westin (ed.), *The Supreme Court: Views from the Inside,* W. W. Norton & Company, Inc., New York, 1961.

No judge likes to be reversed on appeal. Perhaps he likes to be reversed least of all on questions involving basic social values; yet those are the very kinds of cases that are most often accepted by the nation's highest court. Some of these involve interpretation of state statutes and constitutions by the federal high court, and this is especially galling to state judges. Furthermore, the long-range trend has been for the United States Supreme Court to permit expansion of federal activities, bringing about additional resentment from some state judges.

SPECIAL COURTS There are quite a few special-purpose courts in the various states. Perhaps the most common is the probate (or surrogate) court which has the principal responsibility for the probating of wills and the settlement of estates. Juvenile courts and domestic-relations courts are sometimes established as branches of probate courts, or they may be organized separately. These courts have attempted to get away from ordinary judicial procedure and have sought to make extensive use of social workers, psychologists, and other specialists. The goal in using this procedure is to provide constructive assistance rather than to impose penalties.

LOCAL COURTS

THE JUSTICE OF THE PEACE At the grass-roots level the traditional institution for community justice is that of the justice court. This court originated in England and has existed in this country almost without change since colonial times. The justice of the peace (JP) need not be an attorney and probably knows little law, but he is authorized to hear and settle civil actions involving small amounts of money (up to a limit of, say, $500), hold preliminary hearings for felonies, and try minor criminal cases. The JP was once a man of considerable prestige in his neighborhood, but he is not likely to be today. Instead of being a country squire whose "father image" allowed him to dispense a rule-of-thumb justice in neighborhood disputes in an agrarian society with a relatively simple legal system, he is now likely to be some minor local politician of modest social standing.

The office of justice of the peace has been criticized a great deal in recent decades. The fact that the JP is elected by a small constituency, often the township, gives him an opportunity to profit from nonresidents who come before his court, and he may do so with no fear of electoral recrimination. Efforts, successful in some states, have been made to eliminate the justice court. Its presiding officer is normally influential in local politics, however, and the justices frequently have powerful statewide organizations to protect their interests. Despite this, in recent years the character of the office has been changing. In some states, it has lost some of its powers. Many justices are largely inactive and many do not even bother to qualify for office once elected. In the early 1970s, efforts were being made to prohibit JPs from hearing criminal cases on the grounds that nonlawyers were not competent to assure due process of law.

OTHER MINOR COURTS   Although justice courts continue to exist in some urban and especially suburban communities, the tendency is for cities to have their own court systems, generally under names such as "magistrate's court," "traffic court," "court of common pleas," or "police court." These urban courts are usually made up of salaried judges who have legal training and devote full time to the job. However, the pay is likely to be poor, the courts undignified, and the judges not of high quality, although there are probably many exceptions to this generalization. The person of influence is usually treated far differently from a low-status person.

These courts deal particularly with traffic cases but also handle such things as lawsuits or contract violation claims involving a few hundred dollars, violations of building codes and landlord-and-tenant statutes, family disputes, alcoholics, prostitutes, and feuding neighbors, or complaints from mentally disturbed persons who fancy that they have been wronged. In some cases, the judge's ability to serve as a counselor or lay psychiatrist may be more important than his knowledge of the law.

JUDGES AND JURIES

HOW JUDGES ARE CHOSEN   As a result of the nineteenth-century effort to bring government closer to the people, judges were commonly made elective, and their terms were kept of relatively short duration, two or four years. Only in the East, where the pattern of government was well established before the full impact of Jacksonian democracy was felt, was a different method adopted. In those states—and for some courts in other states—most judges are appointed by the governor or elected by the legislature.

Later advocates of reform thought that the practice of electing judges was detrimental to the interests of society. The argument ran that judges should not only be lawyers but should be especially good lawyers, that they should have an understanding of sociology, and that voters were ill-equipped to select them because voters cannot evaluate the qualifications of the candidates. It was pointed out that many persons of low standing in the legal profession were often put forward as candidates by political organizations seeking to repay debts for party service. Appointment by the governor was commonly proposed as a substitute for election.

We now know that no simple formula exists for choosing the best way by which to select judges. Some governors make most of their appointments from among the best attorneys available; others use political party more than professional criteria and therefore sometimes appoint men of poor quality.

Their appointments are, however, subject to the scrutiny and criticism of the bar and this is an inhibiting influence upon them. Where judges are elected, various devices have emerged to help put in office persons who are qualified, at least by the standards of the local bar association. In some cities and states, the bar association makes endorsements or takes a poll on the relative qualifications of various candidates. These endorsements are given wide publicity and are influential in filling positions, particularly if there is no incumbent. Incumbent judges who seek reelection are normally chosen over their challengers because of the greater familiarity of names—and a judge whose incompetence has become notorious risks losing his seat in the next election by that very fact.

Some states have what is nominally an elected, but in reality virtually an appointed, judiciary. Because of the tendency of judges to stay in office until death, promotion, or the infirmities of age force them to retire, they seldom fail to run for reelection. The result is that the governor fills most vacancies in judgeships by appointment. And because the incumbent normally has a great advantage in elections, the new judge is then elected and reelected until he dies, when the governor again fills the post. It is possible for a majority of the judges in a state to have been originally appointed to their posts by the chief executive; the theory thus provides for an elected judiciary, but the practice produces virtually an appointed one with periodic review by the voters.

THE MISSOURI PLAN FOR APPOINTMENTS Since 1937, the American Bar Association has advocated a plan whereby the chief executive appoints each judge from a list prepared by a nominating panel composed of judges and lay persons. At the end of a year or at the next election and periodically thereafter the judge's name would appear on the ballot with the question: Shall Judge Jones be retained in office? If the vote is unfavorable the chief executive must appoint someone else from the nominating panel's list. This plan is likely to have the effect of giving control over judgeships to the state or local bar associations, and some critics have pointed out that this would probably give the bench a conservative and middle-class bias. The plan is in effect in Missouri and Alaska; a somewhat similar plan is used in California as well as in Kansas for the Supreme Court and in a few other cases.

REMOVAL OF JUDGES As with other public officials, means exist for the removal of judges, but seldom are any of these used or even attempted. Perhaps the most common method is rejection at the polls, although even a judge with a bad reputation sometimes encounters little difficulty in securing reelection. Although one might expect that judges would occasionally have to defend specific decisions at election time, this appears to happen rarely. In fact, the public pays little attention to judicial elections.

Judges may also be removed by impeachment, order of the state supreme court or the governor (after a hearing), joint resolution of the legislature, or recall. The rules are different in each state.

TENURE AND QUALIFICATIONS Most states require that judges be "learned in the law," that is, that they be lawyers. This does not apply to the justices of the peace who may be barbers, factory workers, housewives, or almost anything else, including lawyers. North Carolina requires judges to "believe in God"; some other states ask that they be "of good character"; but most make no formal requirement. Terms of office vary from election for two years in the case of some trial courts and of the supreme court in Vermont to appointment for life in Massachusetts.

Unlike the federal court system, each state court is usually autonomous and is coordinated with others only by the general laws of the state and the procedural rules laid down by the state supreme court. The latter may have specific powers of this kind, or it may have influence only through the effect its decisions have upon the lower courts. Frequently one state trial judge works very hard while another loafs; one follows a set of procedures that would not be accepted by the next. New Jersey has a unified court system, and the American Judicature Society has long urged that all inferior courts become branches of a single statewide court system with unified administrative supervision. Some states are moving in this direction.

In traditional legal practice, it has been the job of the judge to decide questions of law, and of the jury to decide questions of fact. The way in which juries do this in practice has often been condemned by both lawyers and laymen who say that these bodies behave with startling inconsistency, that the process is cumbersome and expensive, that jurors are not typical citizens but often ne'er-do-wells picked because they need the extra income, that minority-group persons are often excluded, that working-class persons cannot arrange their jobs to serve, or that jurors cannot understand the technical testimony frequently presented.

Some of these criticisms are probably valid, especially as to the means by which jurors are selected. But the desirability of eliminating the jury because its procedures are not very rational is questionable. Although the method by which the jury reaches conclusions often involves more emotion than logic, it plays an important role in bringing the values of the culture to the judicial process. Undoubtedly jurors sometimes view certain kinds of criminals as heroes, and their attitudes differ with the type of charge. They sometimes are harsh with the one who murders during a family argument—a type of criminal who rarely repeats his crime and is not likely to be dangerous to society—but may sympathetically free a dangerous psychopath. Certainly jurors are likely to be swayed by their emotions and prejudices and may ignore all of the competent technical testimony in favor of these considerations. Yet, in doing this they help keep the law in step with the essentially stable, but nevertheless ever-changing values of society.

SELECTION OF JURORS Persons to be called for service on both grand and petit juries are chosen in a variety of ways depending upon state law. A panel of names of prospective jurors may be drawn from the property tax or voters' lists by the judges, court clerks, jury commissioners, or sheriffs. Although in theory a "jury of one's peers" should contain a broad cross section of society, both the law and the practice of those making selections are such as to exclude many citizens from service, particularly persons who have had an above-average amount of education. It is commonplace to exempt or excuse physicians, lawyers, teachers, and college professors. On the other hand, hourly paid employees must often ask to be excused on the basis of hardship. The nonrepresentative character of the jury is one of the most telling criticisms against it.

In criminal trials before a petit jury, the prosecutor, defense attorney, and judge each have an opportunity to challenge and reject persons whose names are pulled from the "jury wheel" if the person is thought to be prejudiced or to have formed an opinion already or has very much knowledge of the case. The judge may also exclude persons who present a plausible excuse for being "unable" to serve.

THE GRAND JURY This body in common law consisted of from 12 to 23 property owners—today it is sometimes smaller—"to which is committed the duty of inquiring into crimes committed in the county from which its members are drawn, the determination of the probability of guilt, and the finding of indictments against supposed defendants."[5] Traditionally, the grand jury has had two functions: (1) to decide whether persons brought before it by the prosecutor should, according to the evidence presented, be held for trial and (2) to con-

[5] "Grand Jury," *American Jurisprudence,* Lawyers Cooperative Publishing Co., Rochester, N.Y., 1939, p. 832.

duct investigations into the existence of a crime, or of crime generally, and to hold for trial, through a "presentment," persons it believes may be guilty of crimes, even if the prosecutor has not acted.

For the purpose of returning indictments, the grand jury is falling into disuse and about one-half the states place little or no dependence upon it for this purpose. In its native England, the grand jury has been virtually abolished. The indictment was never anything more than a finding by the jury that there was enough evidence to make it probable that the accused is guilty and should be held for trial. Replacing the use of the grand jury in deciding this today is another ancient procedure whereby the prosecutor himself, occasionally in some states and frequently in others, simply files an "information" with the appropriate court saying that he is holding John Soandso for trial, specifying the charge. This method is faster and less expensive than the grand jury method. Prosecutors much prefer it. They dislike having to face two juries, and they prefer not to reveal any of their evidence before the trial, as is necessary to get a grand jury to indict. Although one of the functions of the grand jury is disappearing, that body continues occasionally to perform a vital service as a citizens' investigating body. Whenever the prosecutor is lazy, incompetent, or corrupt, a grand jury may be the only means by which the suspected existence of crime or of maladministration in public office may be inquired into, although sometimes the state attorney general may act where the local prosecutor has failed to do so. Any investigating grand jury can hold persons for trial. It has the power to require the appearance of witnesses, to punish for contempt, and to grant immunity in exchange for testimony that may be self-incriminating.

THE TRIAL JURY The common-law trial jury consisted of 12 persons and a unanimous verdict was required for it to bring in a verdict. It is called the petit (i.e., small) jury to distinguish it from the grand (i.e., large) jury. The tendency today is to use the jury in fewer and fewer cases, turning the more complex ones over to the judge, especially in civil actions. In some states, a criminal defendant may waive jury trial, and the defendant is not in all cases entitled to a jury trial. Other trends include the growing use of a body smaller than 12 and toward a dropping of the requirement for a unanimous decision. The latter is thought by some law specialists to give the defendant an undue advantage and to increase delays and expenses because of the number of hung (undecided) juries.

OFFICERS OF THE COURT   In addition to the judge, who in theory represents the interests of society at large, the court of record has a clerk who prepares the technical documents used in the legal process, keeps the transcript of the court proceedings, and calls witnesses by subpoenas and jurors by summonses. In some states, he has the imposing title of prothonotary. Often he is elected, and he may serve on a fee, rather than salary, basis. The bailiff, commonly a deputy sheriff, serves legal court papers made out by the clerk, has custody of prisoners during trial, and keeps order. Other actors in the courtroom, although they are not officers of the court, include: the prosecuting attorney (his title varies from state to state), who presents the case on behalf of the state; the sheriff, the traditional law enforcement officer of the county; and the coroner, who investigates deaths under unusual circumstances and decides, sometimes with the help of a jury, whether a deceased person died a natural, suicidal, or accidental death or by the "hands of a person or persons unknown."

All these officials are normally elected to office. Because of the technical job he must perform—involving as it does both medical and legal knowledge—there is a trend toward the abolition of the coroner's office and toward turning its functions over to a medical examiner on the prosecutor's staff. There is no trend toward a basic change in any of the other offices.

REVIEW QUESTIONS

1. Describe the organization of the court system of your state.

2. Discuss "justice" as a cultural concept.

3. What have been the criticisms levied against the office of justice of the peace?

4. How does an appellate court differ from a court "of the first instance"?

5. What is meant by the court as "a maker of public policy"?

6. How does the function of the judge differ from that of the jury?

7. Suppose that the Missouri plan for the selection of judges were adopted in your state. What differences would this probably make in the choice of judges, as compared with the present pattern?

8. Why can we not say which plan for the selection of judges is the "best" one?

9. How may judges be removed from office in your state?

10. Describe the method of selection of judges in your state, and evaluate its operation.

11. What is the difference between the function of the grand jury and that of the petit jury?

12. If the behavior of juries is not usually very rational, what is the justification for the preservation of the jury system?

13. Is the cliché, "justice delayed is justice denied" based on fact? Why or why not?

6 LOCAL GOVERNMENT

Unlike the state, the local community is likely, though by no means certain, to have a general set of goals that are dominant and that give it a purpose and life style to which most citizens adhere with a minimum of conflict. The county is probably more likely than is the city, village, or township to have rural-urban and other conflicts as part of its political pattern, but it, too, usually enjoys a considerable degree of citizen agreement as to its purpose.

THE URBAN COMMUNITY

Although the differences between urban and rural life are rapidly disappearing in America, there are still great distinctions between the social, economic, and political interests of, for example, a Chicago suburbanite and corn-hog farmer of central Illinois. Still wider differences exist between these two and those of the small-town merchant in the economically depressed coalfields of the southern part of the state.

These contrasts exist in every state in varying degrees. Because there are so many differences within a single state—differences in ways of earning a living, in rural, small-town, or city dwelling, in racial and ethnic groupings, in religious beliefs, in political party membership—state government policy making tends to be based upon a balancing off of the various effective interests as they bring pressure upon the legislatures, governors, courts, and bureaucracy of the state. There is usually no single, dominant view of what is the desirable and proper function of state government in society. Instead, policy generally represents a compromise among a number of competing and

TABLE 2 Approximate number of local governments in the United States, by type

TYPE OF GOVERNMENT	NUMBER OF UNITS		
	1967	1952	1942
Total	81,298	105,743	155,116
U.S. government	1	1	1
States	50	48	48
Counties	3,049	3,049	3,050
Municipalities	18,048	16,778	16,220
Townships and towns	17,105	17,202	18,919
School districts	21,782	56,346	108,579
Special districts	21,264	12,319	8,299

Source: Based on U.S. Bureau of the Census, *Governments in the United States,* 1967. The definition of special districts was changed between 1952 and 1962 so as to include about 10 percent more agencies within this category.

conflicting interests. Consensus on purpose and direction is lacking; government serves a large number of clientele groups, none of them completely or in the exact manner they would like to be served, but adequately to meet their strongest demands in most cases.

URBAN POLITICAL STYLES

THE LARGE CITY In the largest of our cities, politics resembles that on the state level in the sense that there is a good deal of conflict, and that differences are generally settled not by consensus, but by the balancing of the effective interests in the political process. Disagreements and maneuvering for political advantage in a situation of constantly changing alliances and uneasy compromise are characteristic. Some studies indicate that this is one of the things about the large city that suburbanites most dislike—they feel they already have enough conflict in their lives at home and at work; that local government should serve basically as a consumer service institution providing such things as street lights and fire protection, not as an arena for social or economic reform. In contrast, the disadvantaged ethnic and racial groups of the large city are likely to feel that the principle of "one man, one vote" makes the political system a good one through which to advance their claims of equality and to overcome social and economic deprivations.

THE SMALL TOWN The small town stands in sharp contrast to the large city. Here, something like political consensus is likely to exist because there will often be a minimum of differences in ethnic background and life styles. The most characteristic features of American small-town politics are: (1) a desire to avoid conflict, and (2) a desire to avoid making decisions that would challenge the low-tax ideology that usually prevails. In keeping with the former, the political style of small towns is one of endless discussion, of time-consuming and delicate compromises so that when the governing board finally takes a vote there will be formal unanimity. Because small towns are dominated by small businessmen, their political leaders are concerned about taxes first, services second. The small businessman regards the property tax as a cost of doing business; expanded services therefore threaten profits, and, he fears, possible economic disaster for him. Thus, the small community usually seeks to avoid innovation, strongly opposes the social-service state, and seeks to postpone as many decisions as possible. The adoption of new service programs is rare, reluctant, and regarded with apprehension, in contrast to the middle-sized and large city. In the latter, innovation is encouraged to some degree, at least, and complex programs are carried out by a professional bureaucracy on behalf of an interdependent, impersonal society that feels the need for these programs in order to provide security and a chance for economic and social advancement (neither of which is really possible in the small town).

THE SUBURB Suburbia, in turn, is different from both the large core city and the small town, though it borrows something from each. Like the small-town dweller, the suburbanite is likely to feel close to his government unless he lives in an unincorporated area controlled by the county, to favor policy making by friends and neighbors on a do-it-yourself basis, and to keep the local bureaucracy on an amateur or, if it seems necessary, a semiprofessional basis. Like the core-city dweller, he is likely to want government to provide many services and thus to add to life's amenities as well as to symbolize his own status in life by making his suburb as prestigious as possible. He is willing to pay for these things, but he is also concerned about taxes and aware of his share of them, yet he does not share the low-tax ideology of the villager (although this view does predominate in a minority of suburbs). The suburbanite is likely to be keenly interested in the policies of his community—especially those related to school plant and curriculum, streets, planning, and land-use controls. In this respect, he differs from both his village and large-city contemporaries, for they are likely to be apathetic in their attitudes toward municipal government—the former because there is so seldom an issue to stir up interest, the latter because he sometimes feels that he cannot influence the political process and that he is isolated from the impersonal bureaucracy that carries out its decisions. The suburban movement, whatever short-comings philosophers may find in it, has undoubtedly been a real source of rejuvenation for the grass-roots democracy that has always been thought important by Americans.

IMAGES OF CITY GOVERNMENT

The city and village have always had boundaries that are more purpose-fully drawn than are those of the county, township, or even school district. Until the twentieth century, the limits of municipalities gener-ally advanced with the urbanization of an area, or perhaps just a little ahead of it. But the pattern changed with the development of modern techniques of water supply and sewage disposal which permitted urban life styles to exist beyond the limits of public utilities systems. For a number of reasons, which will be discussed briefly in Chapter 7, citizens preferred to have independent suburbs rather than to join the established city. The result was metropolitan areas made up of a core city and a number—perhaps very many—suburbs.

The city, whether the core or a suburb, develops an identity of its own. Its governmental policies are a reflection of the values and goals of those who are its residents. How do these people view city govern-ment? What do they consider to be the proper functions of their municipality? There are probably many images of local government. Few of them have been identified, but one study has tentatively iso-lated the following images:[1]

1. *The city as an instrument of community growth* Those who see the municipality in this guise believe that it has a duty to help the community to expand in both population and wealth. This is the "boosterism" that is traditional in America, stemming from the frontier notion that growth is progress, bigness is goodness, and that a com-munity must expand or die. The merchant, banker, newspaper editor, chamber of commerce manager, and city bureaucrat all stand to gain from growth, and they are all likely to see the city government's high-est duty as that of furthering it.

The specific policies that a city may pursue as part of a program of boosterism vary with local conditions. Typical activities include the rezoning of land for industrial use, the extension of sewer and water lines to factory sites, efforts at annexation designed to bring potential industrial areas into the city, and low taxes on vacant land zoned

[1] This material borrows from Oliver P. Williams and Charles R. Adrian, *Four Cities,* University of Pennsylvania Press, Philadelphia, 1963.

"industrial" and on new plants. There may be a variety of other activities, too, such as a general program of beautification and of subtle or open advertising of the city as a "center of culture" and a nice place to live.

2. *The city as the provider of life's amenities* In a wealthy nation with a high standard of living, Americans are conscious of themselves as conspicuous consumers. Individual status in an impersonal society is symbolized in large part by the consumption items one can afford. To an increasing extent—above all in suburbia—government is viewed as an agency for providing not merely the necessities of life, but for adding to the comforts of urban living. Supporters of this image of municipal government reject growth as the highest goal, or sometimes as any goal at all. They often prefer the smallness of the suburb to the growing metropolis, and the expenditure of funds in residential neighborhoods to outlays benefiting Main Street.

Those who think the most important job of the municipality is to further the provision of amenities may favor the attraction of industry if they are convinced that it is necessary to give support to the tax base and hence to make possible consumer services that could not otherwise be afforded. But they will be certain to place many restrictions around the development of any but the lightest industry and will be very much interested in land-use controls as a means of shaping the pattern of life that develops in the community. They are also likely to see the avoidance of conflict as itself one of the amenities. They are thus likely to favor the encouragement of the "homogeneity principle"—that is, they will seek to attract to their community only those whose life styles and perhaps ethnic or racial membership are the same as those of the already dominant group. They may think of the best government as being that which is governed by consensus rather than conflict, even though one of the purposes of democracy is to umpire and compromise the conflicts that arise among citizens.

3. *The city government as a caretaker* This is the view of the small-government, low-tax advocate—the conservative. He sees government at all levels as best when it survives at a minimal level, providing only those functions that are ancient or—from his viewpoint—essential. Municipalities may patrol the streets against thieves and purify the water supply, but they should not seek expansion of functions into new areas. The advocate of caretaker government believes that the private allocation of personal resources is invariably to be preferred to governmental allocation. The caretaker view also has an appeal beyond the ideological conservative who prefers minimal government at all levels, to retired persons on fixed incomes, to the marginal homeowner who can barely afford to keep himself in that prestigious category, and to the person whose neighborhood already has a full quota of local services or is better supplied than the poorer or newer areas of the community.

Some suburbs are dominated by the caretaker rather than the amenities philosophy, and this is more likely to be true of working-class suburbs than others. Labor union members, who often support proposals for liberal service programs from the state or federal governments, may take this view if they are homeowners, especially if they fear that they will not be able to continue to own their homes if expensive new programs, requiring large tax increases, are adopted. They may prefer gravel to paved streets, open ditches to curb and gutter, septic tanks to sewers, and individual wells to water-supply systems.

Advocates of caretaker government may oppose not only the amenities concept, but boosterism as well. Marginal homeowners may fear that a policy of wooing new firms will mean generous tax allowances or the extension of municipally owned utilities to new locations at less than full cost to those benefited. The marginal homeowner may see a new plant in his town as nothing more than a threatened increase in his water bill and property tax. The philosophical conservative may oppose boosterism because of the danger that a new firm may bring with it or encourage the establishment of a strong—and politically active—trade union.

4. *The city as arbiter of conflicting interests* Those who hold to this view do not see local government as charged with any single dominant mission; rather they consider it as an umpire with the responsibility to allocate the scarce resources of the community in such a way that all interested groups (in practice, this usually means politically effective groups) get a share. The self-conscious minority-group leaders, seeing no prospect for controlling the local government by themselves or in an effective coalition, are likely to take this point of view.

So did the traditional political boss, whose power depended in part upon satisfying the strongest demands of minority groups. The psychic or numerical majority can realistically advocate a concept of the "general good" or the "public interest," but a permanent minority can seek only access and a set of rules that will help to guarantee it.

All of these images, and others, probably exist in any community simultaneously. Rarely would a community larger than a small town demonstrate such total agreement that a single type would stand in unrivaled control over the minds of policy makers. In most cases, a variety of images serve as frames of reference for officeholders and for citizens as they vote on referendum matters. These ideas about the proper role of municipal government serve to determine the kinds of decisions that are made and the way in which they are made in the contemporary American city.[2]

FORMS OF MUNICIPAL GOVERNMENT

Americans have long been attracted to the idea that there is a close relationship between governmental structure and effectiveness. Many reformers have assumed that all they need do to get the kind of government they want is to find the "right" formal structure and all other questions will take care of themselves. On the basis of what we now know, it would seem that structural arrangements do have an effect upon the quality of government, but they neither guarantee nor prevent good government. The forms of government are important because they affect the pattern of influence of various groups upon policy making. The specific structure in any given case helps to establish behavior patterns and attitudes toward power and the exercise of power that definitely affect the process whereby decisions are made.

There are three basic forms of city government in the United States, the mayor-council, commission, and council-manager plans. There are many variations of each of these and probably no two cities in the nation have exactly the same structure of government. Nearly every

[2] For more on ideologies that have influenced public policy making, see Charles R. Adrian, *State and Local Governments,* 3d ed., McGraw-Hill Book Company, 1971, chap. 2.

charter commission or state legislature, in considering structure, finds it politically expedient to add its own improvisations on the given theme.[3]

THE MAYOR-COUNCIL PLAN　During nearly all of the nineteenth century, American cities were operated under the weak-mayor–council (or weak-mayor) system. Near the end of that century, what is now called the strong-mayor system gradually evolved. In recent years a third principal derivative of the plan, the strong-mayor–council plan with chief administrative officer (or strong mayor with CAO) plan has been developed in order to correct a major weakness of the strong-mayor system in large cities.

The various types of mayor-council cities taken collectively make up more than one-half of all cities of the nation under any form of government. Fifty-two percent of American cities of more than 5,000 population are of the mayor-council types. So are most smaller cities, except in New England, where the town remains the governing body in smaller urban areas. All but six of the twenty-seven cities of more than one-half million use the mayor-council plan, usually of a strong-mayor type. More than one-half of the small cities of 5,000 and 10,000 people have the mayor-council form, usually of a weak-mayor type.

The weak-mayor–council plan　In the early decades of the nineteenth century, America's budding cities borrowed from rural government certain essential concepts. Today the resulting organizational scheme is called the weak-mayor–council plan. As a product of the frontier and a day when municipal functions were simple and few and people were afraid to give powers to a single executive, this plan provided for highly decentralized decision making.

The council is both a legislative and an executive organization under the weak-mayor plan. It may be rather large—up to 50 members, though less than 10 in smaller places—and members are often elected by wards on a partisan ballot. The mayor has few administrative powers. He may preside over the council, and normally has a veto and can recommend legislation. No single individual is charged with

[3] For details on structure, see Charles R. Adrian and Charles Press, *Governing Urban America,* 3d ed., McGraw-Hill Book Company, New York, 1968.

responsibility for seeing to it that the laws and ordinances are properly carried out or that the various municipal activities are coordinated. The principal offices are filled in a variety of ways, by appointment by the mayor or the council, by direct election, or by right of another office (ex officio). Departments are often headed by boards with members having long, overlapping terms and often long tenure in their positions.

Some characteristics of the weak-mayor plan are still to be found in many cities, but relatively few cities of over 50,000 people now use it. In smaller places it remains common. The plan declined in use in the larger places, for which it was never designed, because of its lack of provision for political and administrative leadership or for the coordination of the many activities of such communities. Reformers wanted effective executive leadership and simple, "visible" organizational structure.

The strong-mayor–council plan   This modification of the original plan began to emerge near the end of the nineteenth century. It gradually became more popular, although even today its use remains limited largely to our major cities. Some version of it is to be found in most of the municipalities of more than 500,000 people. The plan calls for the concentration of administrative responsibility in the hands of the mayor, while policy making is a joint function of the mayor and council. The mayor normally prepares the annual budget and administers it once the council adopts its version of it. The mayor has enough administrative power to be able to coordinate the planning of the activities of the various departments and to give some set of priorities to their demands. He also, by this fact, is in a position to exercise strong policy leadership. The council, which usually consists of seven or nine members, plays a subordinate role and members usually serve on a part-time basis. In the postwar years, there has been a tendency, especially in large cities using this plan, to add a chief administrative officer immediately responsible to the mayor. The purpose of this arrangement is to overcome the objection that mayors often have little administrative skill or interest and therefore need a professional administrator who can coordinate the various departments in the important routine of day-to-day administration and who can attend to the details of personnel and budgetary administration. This arrangement frees the mayor for his two other major jobs, those dealing with ceremonial functions and with proposing and launching broad overall policy.

THE COMMISSION PLAN This plan, which was briefly popular around the time of World War I, has been declining in use for several decades. It is characterized by the dual role played by the members of the city council, who are called commissioners. Each of them serves individually as the head of one of the city's administrative departments, while collectively they serve as the policy-making council for the city.

The commission is small, usually consisting of five members. There is a mayor, but he has no powers beyond those of the other commissioners, except that he performs the ceremonial functions and presides over council meetings. He has no veto power. The plan has many weaknesses, especially in the inability of cities to get men qualified to administer complex municipal services to run for offices that usually pay a low salary. It thus produced amateur administration at a time when professional administration was in demand, and it was therefore quickly outmoded, especially by the council-manager plan which began its development about a decade after the commission plan was first launched in Galveston in 1901.

THE COUNCIL-MANAGER PLAN This structural arrangement has become enormously popular since its first use about 1908. By 1962, nearly one-half of the cities of more than 25,000 population had adopted it, and it was especially popular in suburbs and middle-sized cities generally. Its outstanding characteristics include a small council of laymen (usually five to nine members) responsible for policy, and a professional administration under a chief administrator, the manager, who is selected by the council and serves at its pleasure.

The council is usually elected at large on a nonpartisan ballot. Its members serve on a part-time basis and generally rely heavily on the manager for guidance and policy innovation. There is no separation of powers or system of checks and balances as in the mayor-council plan. The mayor normally performs only ceremonial functions and presides over the council. He has no veto power.

The council-manager plan reflects the goals established by the reformers of the second decade of the twentieth century, for they wanted to free councilmen from the petty details of "errand running" for their constituents; they wanted councilmen who would be concerned with the major policies of the community and who would not be parochial in their interests; and they wanted a professional administration to operate the city on a day-to-day basis, a professionalism that would apply to the chief administrator as well as to department heads and general employees. The plan has had special appeal to Americans who have long wanted to remove "politics" from municipal government and to place it on a "businesslike" basis. Of course, politics is essential in a democracy, in the sense that democracy is the process by which popular wants are compromised and converted into public policy by elected officeholders. And there is, of course, politics of this kind in all municipalities. But by relying on the advice of professionals in all branches of municipal government, the council-manager plan appeals to the desire of a great many citizens to minimize political conflict; simultaneously it helps to provide the expertise that they wish to see applied to the complex functions of today's governments. As a result of these appeals to popular wants, the council-manager plan has been used by increasing numbers of communities.

THE COUNTY

Although it often began as a unit of government with the most arbitrary of boundaries, the county prior to the advent of the auto and the telephone was the largest unit of government with which the citizen could hope to have direct, personal contact. Especially in rural areas, a legion of social organizations was established using the county as the area of focus. It became a center for the administration of health, welfare, and educational programs, for the dispensing of justice, for the payment of taxes, for the election of legislative representatives, for the agricultural extension program, for voluntary social agencies, for the county fair, for the keeping of records of births, deaths, land transfers and debts, for the maintenance of roads, and for a thousand other things, governmental and otherwise. The county was not an impersonal administrative unit of the state with meaningless boundaries. It was, instead, a real, an important, social and political center. In rural and small-town areas of the United States, despite changes in our way of life, it remains such today.

THE PURPOSES AND STRUCTURE OF COUNTY GOVERNMENT The traditional functions of the county, mentioned above, carried out what were considered in legal theory to be state responsibilities. The county was only a local agent, carrying on duties that could not, because of time and distance, be handled easily from the state capital. In recent decades, the trend has been toward giving the county additional responsibilities, particularly those that were once thought of as being strictly municipal functions—sewage disposal, water supply, fire protection, planning and zoning, and others.

In general, county government is organized around a governing board and a greatly varied and often complex array of individual officers, boards, commissions, and ex officio bodies. The pattern is not uniform, usually, even within a state. Part of the structure and even many details of organization may be set out in the state constitution. The remainder is usually determined by state law. Traditionally, county governing bodies have had little direct control over the structure of government.

The variation in county governments is indicated by the great variety of names that have been given to governing bodies. Most of them are referred to by titles similar to either board of commissioners or board of supervisors, but some are called levy courts, county courts, fiscal courts, commissioners' courts, commissioners of roads and revenue, and police juries.

Despite the variety, a few generalizations can be made about county government, including the following:

1. With the exception of a very few urban counties, there is no chief executive officer for the county. A group of coequal, elected administrators is the common pattern.

2. County government grew unsystematically and has rarely been deliberately revised and altered as has municipal government in most states.

3. The separation-of-powers principle has not been important in county government. Executive, legislative, and judicial powers are often centered in the same person.

4. County government structure is generally of two types: the commissioner form and the supervisor form. The former centers around a small governing board directly elected by the voters either at large or by districts and with the board members being concerned primarily or exclusively with county government duties. The latter has a governing board, often of much larger size, some or all of whose members serve ex officio as county board members by right of holding some other office, usually as judicial, township, or municipal officers.

THE COMMISSIONER FORM About two-thirds of the counties of the nation have governing boards made up of persons elected specifically to serve on those bodies and with no duties at other than the county level.[4] The board of county commissioners is usually small in size, commonly having three or five members. It may be elected by districts or at large or may be nominated by districts and elected at large. Commissioners are normally chosen from districts much larger than a town or township. Typically, the board has both legislative and administrative powers.

The commissioner form was developed in Pennsylvania and spread westward, as did American frontier migration, typically along the lines of parallel. Thus, Ohio, Indiana, southern Illinois, Iowa, and the Western states generally follow the Pennsylvania tradition.

THE SUPERVISOR FORM The state of New York, which adopted some of the tradition of the New England town but modified it and gave greater emphasis to the county, served as the breeding ground for another kind of county government, the supervisor form. This method of governing the county is to be found in about one-third of the states. Again, the migrants carried the old form of government with them in a westerly fashion, so that the supervisor form is found, in addition to New Jersey, in Michigan, Wisconsin, and northern Illinois.

The supervisor form was characterized by the fact that its governing body was made up of persons who were originally elected as township supervisors and who sat on the county governing board in an ex officio capacity. The size of the board was determined by the number of townships in the county, although in most states the cities are entitled to representation on the board according to a formula determined by state law.

[4] See U.S. Bureau of the Census, *County Boards and Commissions,* 1947.

Because of the ex officio character of board membership under the supervisor form, citizens in these states seem to have been somewhat less aware of county government than are citizens in commissioner-form states. Furthermore, the large size of boards of supervisors encourages the use of the committee system for getting the board's work done, and this removes county government still further from citizen oversight.

In addition to the conventional (New York type) supervisor structure of county government, several variations existed which may be subsumed under this form, since they depended wholly or in part upon ex officio governing boards. In some states a judge, usually a judge of probate, served both as chairman of the county board and as a judicial officer. In most of Kentucky and Tennessee, the other members were the justices of the peace of the county. In Arkansas, and in a few counties elsewhere, a single judge acts both in his judicial capacity and as the lone legislative officer of the county.

The supervisor form of county government has undergone a basic change. The ruling of the United States Supreme Court concerning the necessity of having one man equal to one vote has caused courts to rule that the apportionment of county governing boards must also be based on an equal population principle. The traditional supervisor system has been modified to the point of nonrecognition, except in rural areas. Counties are now governed by boards directly elected by the voters on an equal population basis. But in states with the supervisor tradition, the size of the governing board tends to be larger than in those that have had the commissioner system.

COUNTY ADMINISTRATIVE OFFICERS   County government is characterized by the use of the long ballot. Each of the officials who is elected is independent, by and large, of the county board. The original Jacksonian theory called for coordination through the political party, but the party does not perform this function effectively in the typical county today. That legislative body usually has few, if any, coordinating powers over elective officials.

THE FUTURE OF THE COUNTY   The county has traditionally been a unit of government close to citizens in small towns and on farms, but it has been of secondary importance to persons living in cities. For them, the municipal government has been the principal decision-making center and the focus of local politics. With this the case, it might be assumed that the county would decline in importance at a time when the great majority of Americans live in urban areas. Such is not the case, however. In metropolitan areas, counties are engaged in an increasing number of activities of government that traditionally have belonged to the municipality, in particular health, welfare, sewage disposal, and water-supply functions. In addition counties have since the 1930s performed most of the functions formerly administered by townships in states where that unit of government was once important.

The county, in other words, has been undergoing a transition in the last generation and changes in its responsibilities are still being made. Instead of dying as the pattern of life that helped create it disappears, the county is becoming an increasingly important unit for the provision of social services wanted by what is now essentially an urban public. In metropolitan areas of the type to be discussed in the following chapter, it is becoming the principal unit for the provision of area-wide services. It is far more acceptable to the general public than is any other general form of metropolitan government. On the other hand, the fact that the county is a traditional form of government tends to keep its structure rather highly resistant to change. It remains, in most cases, without a chief executive, a career civil service under a merit system, or a representative popular assembly based on the population distribution found in contemporary urban living patterns.

TOWNS AND TOWNSHIPS

THE TOWN The county is an intermediate unit of government for the most part. In the East and Midwest, as well as in some other parts of the country, there is normally a local unit of government closer to the people than the county. The oldest of these is the New England town, a unit of government unique to its part of the nation. These units, each of which originally constituted a church congregation, were natural governmental areas. The term "town" came to mean the entire community, rural and urban land alike. Although the towns were not incorporated, they were recognized by the legislature as having a right to exercise certain powers which elsewhere came to be associated with the municipal corporation and were units of representation in the legislature. As some areas became increasingly urbanized, the town continued to serve as the basic unit of local government. At the time of the War for Independence, there was not a single municipal corporation in New England. Even today, though some modification is taking place, the town remains the common unit of local government in New England.

The town is governed by a meeting of all the qualified voters, who choose officers and make basic policy. There is an annual meeting, traditionally in March, with as many other meetings as may be necessary. After making basic policy, the people choose a board of selectmen, usually three but in some places as many as nine. A fairly large number of other officers—a clerk, treasurer, assessor, overseer of the poor, constable, school committee, and fence viewer—are either elected or appointed by the selectmen. The selectmen and elective officers are then entrusted with carrying out the basic policies established by community action.

The urbanization of many towns has been accompanied by a sharp decrease in attendance at town meetings and a consequent decline in the democratic effectiveness of this form of government. In many areas of New England, a *representative* town meeting plan has been developed. Under this plan, the voters choose a large number of citizens, sometimes as many as one hundred or more, to attend the meeting, represent them, and vote. Any citizen can attend and take part in debates, but he no longer has a direct vote.

TOWNSHIPS In the Middle Atlantic states and in the Midwest, townships developed as basic units of rural government. Rapid means of transportation and communication have made the township less important today than it formerly was, and it has declined in most states where it once existed. It remains active for some purposes, however, in the Middle Atlantic states and in all parts of nine Midwestern states. Scattered townships are also to be found in a few other states, but those that once flourished in Iowa and Oklahoma have been deactivated. In contrast to the general pattern, urbanized townships in Kansas, Michigan, New Jersey, New York, and Pennsylvania are becoming increasingly important as the result of their being given municipal functions to perform.

Township government is organized largely along the lines of the

New England town; many of the states even retain the town meeting which the early settlers carried with them. The annual meeting has fewer powers than in New England, but it usually has the right to levy taxes, approve a budget, adopt such ordinances as state law permits, and to a lessening degree today, elect officers. The states that borrowed from the Pennsylvania pattern have never used the annual meeting. The administrative officers of the township, if not chosen in annual meeting, are nearly all elected at the polls.

THE DECISION MAKERS

The political process involves a number of interrelated parts. The structure of *form of government* makes a difference as to the kinds of policies that are adopted because the particular form in use permits patterns of access that might be different if another form were to be used. *Value systems* are also important to the process, for they tell us which political goals and programs are "right" and which are "wrong." A third significant part deals with interests and the interest groups that are organized around them. American democracy is based in considerable part on the notion that "the squeaking wheel gets the grease," so that the way in which interests act affects the details of public policy (see Chapter 7). But these parts alone do not explain how public policy is formulated. Political leadership draws together the whole process. The individuals who provide it guide interest groups and effect compromises among them. They manipulate value symbols to gain support for their goals from among the rank and file of the citizenry. To them, the legally established structure of government may be either an asset or a liability; if it tends to be the latter, they seek to find particular characteristics of the structure that can be used to advantage, or they may seek to change it so as to strengthen the cause they represent. The political system is not an automated machine. The type and quality of leadership it has affect the nature of the policies of government which are its end product.

COMMUNITY LEADERSHIP Not enough is yet known about those who are discovered in studies to be the "leaders" of the community. It is possible, for example, that persons who appear to be policy leaders, even to the extent of seemingly dominating the decisions of those holding public office, are really only verbalizers. That is, they merely express, as symbolic leaders, the ideas that are already widely accepted in the community. If this is true, the same policies might have resulted whether or not these persons had taken any action in seeking to have policies developed. Leading bankers, merchants, realtors, and chamber of commerce secretaries are certain, in small towns or middle-sized cities, to have their remarks given considerable publicity through newspapers, radio, and television and may thus seem to be real leaders. Merchant princes and bankers are sometimes listened to because they are natural leaders or because of the deference they receive as a result of their prestigious positions. But their preferences as to public policy may be forestalled, for example, by implacable resistance from workingmen responding to a labor leader. This leader's own status position will probably be a modest one, and his technique not one of oppressive coercion but merely of pointing out to the union membership the consequences for them of a proposed line of action.

Yet leadership is an intrinsic part of group existence, and leaders make decisions. Furthermore, group action generates power. Those who take a positive interest in any problem are likely to have a considerable advantage over those who are passive and apathetic. And, of course, those who feel they have the most at stake are also likely to be the ones who become the most active in political decision making.

If leadership were absolute, there would probably be consensus and little community conflict; only a disgruntled few would resist. In most cases, however, leaders have to do more than make a decision and launch a selling campaign. They must overcome opposition from competing leaders. A small amount of knowledge and drive—with a purpose—can sometimes project a relatively low-status person into a leadership position. He finds power in the community unused and seeks to exploit it. When he does so, his action spurs dominant leaders into counterattack. A conflict ensues that may not only get out of control for the initiators of action, but may bring back memories of countless old (and often irrelevant) conflicts from the community's past.

THE POWER STRUCTURE The following points might be kept in mind in regard to the political power structure as it exists or is supposed to exist:

1. Some economically powerful leaders, in particular the managers and top executives of local plants of nationwide corporations, may refuse to become involved in community activities of any kind not directly affecting the company, lest enemies be made unnecessarily. Thus some persons who, because of great economic power, might be expected to be important decision makers exert little or no influence on decisions regarding community public policy. Heads of locally owned firms, however, are likely to be both active and powerful locally.

2. Power structures may not necessarily be constructed in the shape of pyramids, although some studies have found such shapes. It is quite possible to have power structures that do not lead to a few top leaders but instead have a many-centered structure with numerous leaders, each of whom is powerful in some particular area of public policy but not in all such areas. In other words, there may be functional specialization, so that a man who is very influential in deciding questions dealing with, say, traffic-flow patterns may have much less to say about housing policies and may not be consulted at all relative to the introduction of a new recreation program.

3. Some studies show that there are a few people who are very much interested in, and influential over, virtually all important decisions made in regard to public policy. These are the top members of the power elite. It is possible, even probable, that no such small clique of general leaders exists in the largest cities simply because of the great complexity of social organization in large governmental units. In such cities, the leaders in various areas of community policy making seek their own goals, with imperfect coordination of their efforts with those of other leaders seeking other goals. Communication—keeping other leaders and the public informed—becomes increasingly imperfect as the size of community increases. To the public, interest groups, as such, become more visible than the individual leaders as the size of the city increases.

4. Policy leadership should not be confused with policy invention. The studies made so far tend to show that leaders need not themselves be creative in finding solutions to social wants. Their job is to assess proposals as to their degree of adequacy as solutions and then to push for the adoption of those found most acceptable. New ideas in meeting problems are most likely to come from persons with exceptional technical knowledge of a particular subject, persons who may be in the bureaucracies of private business, in government, in the universities, or elsewhere. Their names are commonly little known to the general public and sometimes even to the person who serves as symbolic leader for the promotion of the ideas they have put forth.

5. Governmental officials may once have been tools of the economic leadership group, but they are becoming increasingly important centers of power in their own right; this is especially true as government plays an ever greater role in the lives of citizens. In earlier times, government was simple and performed few functions. With business institutions overwhelmingly important by comparison, business leaders sometimes used officeholders as their front men. This is less likely to happen today, and many important community leaders now themselves become councilmen and mayors. Local politicians today generate demand, mobilize support, and otherwise serve as leaders and are themselves power centers.

6. The top members of the power structure may be powerful because they come from high-status families to whom deference has always been paid by other residents of the community or because they are newspaper editors. But they are most likely to be powerful because they are spokesmen for interest groups and have the ability to bring some of the weight of the group to bear upon political institutions. One's place in the power structure reflects, except perhaps in small cities and towns where individuality remains especially important, the relative overall strength of the groups for whom the leader is a spokesman.[5]

REVIEW QUESTIONS

1. How have the activities of the county changed over the years?

2. Describe the organizational structure of your county. What is the title of the person (or persons) who performs the executive function?

[5] For bibliography on material in this section, see *Governing Urban America,* chap. 5. Research findings relative to community power structure and decision making are analyzed and abstracted in Charles Press, *Main Street Politics,* Institute for Community Development and Services, Michigan State University, East Lansing, Mich., 1962.

3. Why have the functions and characteristics of towns and townships changed in the twentieth century? In what way have they changed?

4. What are likely to be the principal differences between politics in the large city and in the small town?

5. Which of the images of the community do the leaders of your home town most closely follow?

6. Which of the images of the community would you like to see followed in the community in which you may choose to live in the future? Why?

7. Why is it difficult to generalize about the forms of city government in the United States?

8. Explain some of the reasons why the mayor-council form of the nineteenth century has been passing from favor. What are the characteristics of the forms that have been replacing it?

9. What form of government does your home town have? How has its structure changed during its history?

10. Compare the weaknesses in each of the three basic forms of city government. How important are these weaknesses?

11. What factors have contributed to the popularity of the council-manager plan?

12. What is meant by urban power structure? Describe some of the different patterns that are found in it.

7 SOME PATTERNS OF STATE AND LOCAL POLITICS

Politics on the state and local scenes operates largely in the same manner as it does for the selection of congressmen and Presidents and in determining national policies. Only the emphasis and the relative balances of forces are changed. These changes can be important, however, and can make a considerable difference as to the ease or difficulty with which a particular individual or group contacts those who make the important decisions in government. Some of these differences deserve brief attention here, but what follows is not an attempt to describe politics at the state or local level. Rather, the section below introduces some factors that need to be considered in addition to and in connection with those discussed in general descriptions of the American political system if we wish to understand the way in which state and local politics is related to, but differs from, national politics.

DIFFERENCES IN
THE GROUND RULES

FINANCES   The marginal cost of new or expanded programs is greater at the state and local levels than at the federal. Their tax structures are fairly rigid and they cannot borrow money so easily as can the federal government. Many of them have strict rules against going into debt. Their tax receipts do not generally expand with the economy to the degree that federal receipts do. They fear tax competition from other states, for low-tax promises are regarded as helpful in luring industry from one state to another. The result is that the anguished effort required for states and communities to increase their taxes tends to encourage a conservative view on spending. Innovations, if they involve a new expenditure, are thus more commonly products of the federal government.

LEGAL RESTRICTIONS   The federal government has few constitutional restrictions limiting its decisions, except in the area of civil rights. The states and communities, on the other hand, can operate only within the limits of both state and federal constitutions. And the state constitutions are nearly all lengthy documents, containing dozens of restrictions upon decision makers. Local governments are even more hemmed in. They are limited by their charters or by state statutes, and the courts consistently interpret their grants of power in a narrow fashion. Furthermore, they cannot do anything the state cannot do. The greater flexibility of the federal government encourages policy development at that level.

WORKING-CLASS POLITICS: NATIONAL AND LOCAL   The policies favored by both conservatives and liberals do not vary significantly by level of government when the national and state arenas of decision making are compared. Their interests and political behavior are about the same at each level. There is a considerable difference, however, when this behavior is compared with that in the local arena. Working-class people strongly tend to support what are usually called liberal policies at the state and national levels. If they are unionized and their unions have strong social-action programs, this is especially likely to be the case. But a different pattern emerges at the local level, where a large percentage of working people are homeowners and where local revenues are derived mainly from taxes on property. Here we frequently find working people aligned with the most conservative members of the lower middle class in support of caretaker policies. They often want expanded governmental programs at the higher levels where the tax burden is obscure or is thought to fall on others, but will oppose new services at the local level, sometimes even in the face of the urgings of union leaders. Urban renewal is a good example of this, where businessmen's interest groups have opposed federal action before Congress, and liberals including labor union spokesmen have favored it. But at the local level, businessmen who are worried about the future of the central business district have favored federal aid as necessary to get projects going, while the people in the areas to be renewed—most of them liberal voters in national elections— drag their feet for fear that displacement will cause them to lose contacts with old friends, to give up an accustomed way of life, and to pay higher rents. As a result of this pattern, there is no clear-cut liberal constituency at the local level to parallel that at state and national levels.

ONE-PARTYISM Many United States senators are elected from one-party states and congressmen from one-party districts. But Congress as a whole is organized on a two-party basis and issues before that body are presented to the American public as being divided along party lines, even though the real line between Republicans and Democrats is, in fact, often hazy. The grandest prize of all, the Presidency, is of course always fought for along party lines.

The picture at the state and local level is much more obscure as to the role of party. Although it is not generally possible for a citizen to go to the polls and elect a *program* for federal governmental action, he is usually even less guided at the other levels. Municipal elections, in a majority of cities, school districts, and in some other jurisdictions, exclude national party activities in both theory and practice. Even where this is not the case, the party label for these elections is likely to be much less important than such things as personal reputation and familiarity of name.

State electoral contests, similarly, do not generally divide on party lines. Fewer than one-fourth of the states have vigorous competition between parties where each has a chance to win in any given state-wide election. The other states have an overwhelmingly dominant party which may be divided up in many different ways. It may consist of two factions (liberal and conservative), or of many factions, or it may consist of a considerable number of largely independent politicians who form uneasy and temporary coalitions. The primary for the governorship is sometimes a free-for-all and the legislature may be an unorganized group of individuals. Under the circumstances, it is often more difficult for the citizen to understand state—and in the more populous jurisdictions, local—politics than national politics. The concept of responsibility and accountability for action is probably more obscure and complicated at these levels than it is for the federal government.

OTHER DIFFERENCES   Other factors also distinguish the rules of the political game at the state and local levels from those at the federal level. State legislatures, for example, have more difficulty than Congress in performing the essential roles of debate, criticism, and modification of executive or bureaucratic proposals, because most of them lack the staff that helps make Congress effective in these roles. The individual amateur in the legislature does not usually have his own group of experts to cross-check the recommendations of the bureaucracy and the lobby. Furthermore, most states, many cities, and the vast bulk of our counties have a civil service that is regarded by specialists as inferior to that of the federal government. This factor tends to cause the professional workers in various fields (e.g., social welfare, public health, highways) to place greater trust in the federal bureaucracy than in those of the lower levels, for they are confident that its members will be committed to the furthering of professional standards and goals.

All these factors modify state and local politics, giving it a character of its own, even while preserving it as a part of the overall American political pattern.

INTEREST GROUPS AND THEIR GOALS

Interest-group characteristics and procedures are discussed in another volume in this series.[1] Some differences exist between levels of government and between particular states or cities, because the relative balance of power varies under different circumstances. On the national and state levels, for example, agricultural groups tend to be powerful. Liquor lobbyists tend to have more influence before state and local bodies than before the national government. Real estate groups and downtown merchants are often extraordinarily powerful in city politics. This is so because groups concentrate on the decision-making centers that most affect them.

The relative strength of any given lobby varies from time to time. Thus, in prosperous times, people may accept much leadership from, and make many concessions to, the business community. In a depression, business groups lose status and hence political strength. Both liquor lobbies and their temperance opponents have relatively less political strength today than they once had, probably because public values change over the years and the resultant change in attitudes affects their lobbying strength.

The pattern of interest-group strengths varies from state to state. In some places, a single group seems to dominate the scene, but the group may be different in each state. In others, two very strong groups may be closely balanced and the pattern of conflict on many issues may reflect the struggle between these groups. In still others, many groups may be closely balanced and domination depends upon the nature of the issue.

SOME PATTERNS A good bit of contemporary conflict before legislatures and state administrative agencies centers around rural and urban differences (over the distribution of the local share of the state

[1] Hugh Bone and Austin Ranney, *Politics and Voters,* 3d ed., McGraw-Hill Book Company, New York, 1971.

gasoline tax between rural and urban units of government, for example). Sometimes it is a split between a huge metropolis and the rest of the state, as between Chicago and downstate, or New York City and upstate.

Conflict between the conservative, prosperous old aristocracy and the small farmers is common in the South, as in Mississippi in the historic struggle between the planters of the delta and the "rednecks" of the hills. In Minnesota many issues center around a split between the conservative and prosperous corn-hog farmers of the southern part of the state and the less well-endowed, liberal-to-radical wheat and potato farmers of the Red River Valley. In New Mexico both cultural and economic interests are symbolized in the friction between "Anglos" and Spanish-Americans, in Louisiana between Catholic French and Protestant Anglo-Saxons, in Massachusetts between late-immigration Catholics and old-family Yankee Protestants, or in New Hampshire between Yankee Protestants and Catholic French-Canadian newcomers. In cities, the conflicts are likely to be between the downtown businessmen and the leaders of organized labor. But they may instead be between those who want the city government to take the lead in a program of boosterism and those who want to protect the neighborhood merchant or who want to further the goals of the homeowners. Or it may be between the advocates of either boosterism or the provision of life's amenities and those who advocate caretaker government and see the most important objective as being that of keeping the city budget from increasing. The pattern is enormously varied at both the state and local levels.

It is not possible here to give a summary of the interests of even the most common and powerful groups. But a list of the major types of interests that are usually represented before state and local governments would include the following: chambers of commerce and manufacturers' associations, banks, downtown-merchants associations, public utilities, railroads, truckers, taxicab companies, insurance companies, general contractors, the professions (lawyers, physicians, dentists, teachers, and others), realtors, liquor and race-track interests, newspapers, general labor-union organizations and their various subdivisions, racial, ethnic, and religious group organizations, public employees, government officials, veterans, groups representing agricultural, conservation and highway interests, and good-government and reform groups.

In addition to the groups representing the major pressures, legislative bodies are intermittently subjected to the idiosyncratic behavior of the extreme left and right fringes of the political continuum and to the loud and insistent demands of crackpots and sensationalists. There appears to be an inexhaustible supply of voluntary groups in America, and each seems to have an interest in influencing public policy.

THE POLITICAL PARTY

Political parties, including those at the state and local levels, are the subject of another volume in this series.[2] These structures are especially important in state politics because American parties are organized on a federal basis, that is, the national parties are loose affiliations of 50 state party organizations and the contests for the prizes of state and federal offices are closely tied together.

Local elections are often tied into the regular party activities, too. But the outstanding characteristic of most city and school district contests is the fact that they are in theory and, in most cases, in practice conducted as "nonpartisan" contests. That is, no party label appears on the ballot, the party organizations normally are not involved in the elections, and candidates must secure their financial and worker support on an individual basis, or as a member of a strictly local party. Although in New York and Chicago parties are deeply involved in municipal politics, in some other large cities, such as Detroit and Los Angeles, they are normally not, and in more than 60 percent of the cities of more than 5,000 population, the party label does not appear on the ballot.

Nonpartisanship was a part of the reform movement program, for it was widely believed in the early part of the present century that national party programs had nothing to do with municipal issues and that professional politicians should, as far as possible, be excluded from local elections where a "businesslike government" was wanted. Probably more than 80 percent of the suburbs incorporated since the end of World War II have provided for nonpartisan elections where state law permits.

[2] *Ibid.*

AN EMERGING DECISION-MAKING ARENA: THE METROPOLIS

The metropolitan area is not a unit of local government, and hence was not considered in the previous chapter. But it is the area where most Americans, and each year an increasing number of Americans, live. Because all areas that are continuously urban have some service and planning problems in common, the metropolis is becoming ever more important as an arena for decision making.

Political disputes have traditionally been concentrated in the national, state, or the local level. With the coming of the suburban movement after World War I, and especially after World War II, this relatively simple arrangement ceased to be adequate. People began to concentrate in ever larger numbers in relatively small geographic spaces, but city boundaries did not expand as fast as did urban populations. The resulting conflicts of interests and demands for service have come to be referred to as "metropolitan-area problems."

THE SUBURB America has changed in a few generations from a land of farmers to one of big-city people. Between the Civil War and 1900, the population of the cities doubled; in the next 25 years it doubled again. By 1920, more than one-half (51.2 percent) of the American people lived in urban areas. The urbanizing trend developed so rapidly that by 1970 about two-thirds of our people lived not only in urban, but in *metropolitan* communities. That is, they lived in areas that had core cities of at least 50,000 people. The greatest gains in population between 1950 and 1970 were in the *suburbs* of metropolitan areas, and it is there that future increases will be concentrated.

As the metropolitan population has increased, so has the number of suburbs. In 1911 eight incorporated municipalities existed in St. Louis County. In 1935 the number had increased to 25; in 1956 it stood at 96. The pattern was much the same around all large cities and was imitated to a lesser extent around the nation's middle-sized cities. The result was an enormous increase in the complications involved in supplying urban services. Not only were huge numbers of people involved, but so were many governmental units. With most suburbanites demonstrating a strong determination to remain independent of the central city, the problem was one of finding ways of coordinating the activities of many different units and of financing the many demands of citizens in a variety of types of suburbs with widely divergent tax resources.

People move to the suburbs for many reasons. In the early days of the movement—from the 1890s through the 1930s—they left the core city largely, though not exclusively, because they were well-to-do, and high status was attached to the person who could say that he was a commuter on the 5:15. In the 1950s and since, people have moved largely in order to reach the available building space. Americans have always shown a sharp preference for the single-family home and in the prosperous years after World War II, this preference with the extensive use of land that it implies, drove builders to the urban fringe. Citizens did not object very strongly to the disadvantage of commuting, for the automobile had made it possible and the telephone had made it convenient. Furthermore, suburbia offered a nice compromise between what people like about the city and what American tradition honored about the small town. Living there one could have the income potential of the city, together with its varied amusements and its specialized services, and at the same time have the advantages that are believed to exist in the suburbs: one's own home, garden, and play yard, lower taxes, and less dirt, noise, congestion, and traffic.

The result of the multiplicity of separate governments in the metropolitan area is a great collection of decision-making problems dealing with providing water supply, sewerage, rubbish and sewage disposal, commuter highways, schools, public health activities, and others, often necessarily on an intergovernmental basis with two or sometimes many governments involved. In addition, independent suburbs create problems in long-range, coordinated planning, effective controls over the use of land and physical facilities, uneven tax resources and assessment practices, and others.

METROPOLITAN GOVERNMENT Many of the techniques available for providing the levels of service expected by the public and the financial base needed to make them possible presume an organizational area that is neither statewide nor simply that of the core city. A variety of intermediate-level governments have been proposed as a result. These include (1) use of the county as an "upper-tier" unit; (2) use of single- or multipurpose special districts with metropolitan-wide boundaries; (3) a "federal" plan, which would leave the core city and its suburbs intact but would relieve them of some of their responsibilities, which would be assigned to a metropolitan-area government; or (4) simple annexation of all urbanized land to the core city, eliminating both incorporated and unincorporated suburbs.

None of these proposals, except for the single-purpose special district (to provide, for example, water supplies, or sewage disposal systems), has proved politically popular. This is not because there are no metropolitan-wide problems. Core cities, which have the highest costs of operation, are suffering from declining tax bases, and their residents feel that they are forced by circumstances and sometimes by law to subsidize the suburbanites (as in letting them use streets for commuting, or parks for recreation); the suburbs have enormous "getgoing" costs, and those must be provided even though some suburbs are rich while others have very little in the way of a tax base; and the suburbs are often said to be guilty of wasteful duplication, providing a poor quality of service, trying to operate with amateur and perhaps incompetent administrators, and of failing to cooperate with other units of government. Some reformers have argued that these problems—they differ greatly from one metropolitan area to another—are sufficient reason to make drastic changes in the way in which our large urban complexes are ruled. But these arguments have had little public support. There are historical and ideological reasons why this is so.

THE DEMAND FOR INDEPENDENCE The politically atomized pattern of contemporary American suburbia results from the fact that this was a rural nation in the days when laws of annexation and attitudes toward large cities were developing. The small-towners who dominate legislatures have for the most part kept the traditional legal situation unchanged. As a consequence, the boundaries of a city are almost always artificial and arbitrary, and have nothing to do with economic and social realities.

Not only has the population of fringe areas grown rapidly, but the number of suburbs has been increasing at a great pace. As each group of subdivisions becomes partially populated, it tends to seek incorporation for itself rather than annexation to another suburb or the core city.

Why do people want "their own" little suburb? A major reason is surely a desire to own their own homes, however heavily mortgaged. Because the cost of home ownership is increased by core-city taxes levied in order to provide urban services, suburbanites hope to be able to afford to own a home by keeping taxes low. Since many suburbanites may feel that they literally cannot continue to afford a home in the price category they are in if costs increase, they will fight anything that threatens higher costs, including taxes. This attitude, therefore, produces hostility toward annexation. It may also produce opposition to the incorporation of the suburb, for incorporation symbolizes increased taxes and the threat of being required to accept urban service costs.

Another significant reason deals with the common belief that the core city is run by professional politicians, is expensive to operate, and is strife-ridden. The first of these is regarded as bad because it violates the Jacksonian value of government by neighbors. The second runs counter to the citizen's use of his home as a status symbol which causes him to prefer patios or home freezers to additional but not very visible services. The last violates a desire for a sense of community, a consensus of values such as existed in rural areas of an earlier day. The core city is made up of many ethnic and racial groups, a variety of subcultures. The one-class, one-culture, one-group tendency in individual suburbs appeals to the desire of the citizen to minimize social tensions and conflicts.

Government in the suburb is also likely to be more personal. One may easily come to know the suburban officials personally or by reputation. The city hall is more personalized and humanized than in the core city. All of these features are regarded as desirable by the typical suburbanite.

THE DESIRE FOR ACCESS A psychological factor that has contributed to the balkanization of the suburbs is the desire of citizens to have access to the decision-making centers of local government. As urban life became more impersonal with the growth of population and as the old-fashioned political machine, which had served as an access point to great numbers of citizens, declined, the feeling of isolation and of frustration on the part of the urbanite must have increased. The reform-period practice of electing all councilmen at large contributed to the barrier that the ordinary citizen saw as being dropped between himself and those who decided things that mattered. But in the suburb, he found a reestablishment of the close relationships that symbolized democracy on the frontier. After he moved to the suburb, the citizen did not necessarily participate more by voting or attending meetings, and he did not make a greater effort to know his governmental officials, but he regained the comfortable feeling that goes with confidence in the thought of having influence over government decisions and of having officeholders who share one's social values.[3]

WHAT KIND OF GOVERNMENT FOR THE METROPOLIS? Politics can be understood only if we remember that in politics we are constantly dealing with distinctions in shades of gray, not with simple blacks and whites, and that, furthermore, there are many sides—not merely two—to every political question. The picture in metropolitan areas clearly demonstrates this. It is not possible to say that those who want a single government for each metropolitan area are right and those who want to continue to have many small governments are wrong, or vice versa. Given their particular sets of values, each group has a plausible case. Sometimes the arguments support one side, sometimes the other. Often they balance in the gray area in between. Reformers, for example, have probably placed excessive emphasis upon an assumed need for neatness in metropolitan-area organization, and upon the goals of efficiency and economy. On the other hand, suburban leaders have often been parochial and short-sighted in viewing public policies.

One scholar-practitioner who has spent much of his lifetime in studying government in metropolitan areas has concluded:

> Our approach, our theory, was wrong. ... We relied on local initiative when we should have known that such initiative is effectively disqualified outside its own established community. ... We lectured business leaders, minority groups, professional politicians, and class-conscious suburbanites on their duty to be "rational" and to support "efficiency," without understanding that these groups each have solid selfish reasons for keeping the

---

[3] For supporting data, see John C. Bollens and Henry J. Schmandt, *The Metropolis*, 2d ed., Harper & Row, Publishers, New York, 1969, especially chap. 16.

present structures. . . . We prayed for "metropolitan leadership" to guide us into the promised land, forgetting that political leadership is firmly tied to a political constituency in being. . . . Finally, it must be admitted, we thought that the metropolitan problem was much simpler than it is and that it could be "solved" by setting up one nice new piece of local government machinery.[4]

Even if we were of a mind to reject most of the conflict discussed above as not dealing with fundamental problems that are considered important by those living in metropolitan areas, we would be left with a number of vitally important concerns that must be faced on an area-wide basis. Unsafe sewage-disposal practices in any part of the area may endanger health in another part. Economics may dictate a collective effort to secure additional water supplies from a distant lake or mountain stream. Traffic-flow patterns for the entire area are necessarily interrelated. Land-use practices in any one section will affect those in other sections. Neither smoke and noise nuisances nor disease germs honor legal boundaries.

These are some of the collective problems. Little agreement exists as to which are the most important, and they probably differ from one metropolitan area to another according to local values and existing service levels. The greatest problem of all, perhaps, is "the inability of metropolitan residents to reach any substantial degree of consensus as to what should be done . . . about the generally recognized issues of their common life—government organization, finance, blight and redevelopment, schools, race relations, land-use control, and so on."[5]

CLOSING STATEMENT

American state and local governments have been romanticized, spoken of in awe and with nostalgia, viewed with alarm, and seen as institutions passing into final eclipse. It is probably safe to discard the extreme points of view. State and local governments are likely to be

[4] Luther Gulick, *The Metropolitan Problem and American Ideas*, Alfred A. Knopf, Inc., New York, 1962, pp. 101–102.

[5] Coleman Woodbury, "Great Cities, Great Problems, Great Possibilities?" *Public Administration Review*, vol. 18, p. 339, Autumn, 1958.

important for the future in the provision of services to people and in the making of policy decisions about those services. These governments will not receive the attention accorded to the federal government, or even that given the United Nations, but they will be important institutions in American society. It is perhaps especially important that they will continue to offer the citizen an opportunity close to his home to participate in government and its political process. The governments that are physically closest to the people, despite all the changes in the means of transportation and communication, remain those most easily available to the citizen who wishes to become active in the tasks of helping to shape the ways of our democracy.

This brief study has sought to describe state and local governments as a part of an interrelated American political process. Some major comparisons and contrasts have been made both in terms of institutions and of the pattern of politics. The reader, if he wishes to assume the responsibilities of citizenship, will want to learn more, not necessarily of isolated facts, but of the process by which state and local offices get filled and decisions about public policy get made. The citizen's opportunities for influencing policy increase as his understanding of the process of politics expands.

REVIEW QUESTIONS

1. How does the balance of forces differ between the federal and the state-local levels of government?

2. Describe some of the major interest groups affecting policy making in your state. Which of them reenforce one another? Which compete? In what ways?

3. Is the nonpartisan ballot used in your city or school district? If it is, do the national parties play any part in these local elections?

4. Why is there a "metropolitan-area problem"?

5. Why do most suburbanites prefer independence from the core city?

6. Discuss some of the advantages you would expect to find for yourself in suburban living. What advantages might you find in a core city of 60,000? Of 1,000,000? What disadvantages might you find in suburban living?

7. Are there problems of suburban–core city conflict in your home-town area? To what extent have past problems been worked out? How? What proposed solutions have been presented to meet current problems?

8. Describe some of the major interest groups affecting policy making in your home town; in the total metropolitan area around your home town. How does the balance of political power differ between that which exists in the core city and that for the metropolitan area as a whole?

FOR FURTHER READING

Adrian, Charles R.: *State and Local Governments: A Study in the Political Process,* 3d ed., McGraw Hill Book Company, New York, 1971.

——— and Charles Press: *Governing Urban America,* 3d ed., McGraw-Hill Book Company, New York, 1968.

Banfield, Edward C.: *The Unheavenly City,* Little, Brown and Company, Boston, 1970.

Bollens, John C., and John C. Ries: *The City Manager Profession,* Public Administration Service, Chicago, 1969.

——— and Henry J. Schmandt: *The Metropolis,* 2d ed., Harper & Row, Publishers, Incorporated, New York, 1969.

Book of the States, Council of State Governments, Chicago, biennially.

Dixon, Robert G., Jr.: *Democratic Representation,* Oxford University Press, Fair Lawn, N.J., 1968.

Jewell, Malcolm: *The State Legislature,* Random House, Inc., New York, 1962.

Jones, Victor: "Local Government in Metropolitan Areas," in Coleman Woodbury (ed.), *The Future of Cities and Urban Redevelopment,* University of Chicago Press, Chicago, 1953.

Key, V. O., Jr.: *American State Politics,* Alfred A. Knopf, Inc., New York, 1956.

Martin, Roscoe C.: *The Cities and the Federal System,* Atherton Press, New York, 1965.

Masters, Nicholas A., Robert H. Salisbury, and Thomas H. Eliot: *State Politics and the Public Schools,* Alfred A. Knopf, Inc., New York, 1964.

Municipal Year Book, International City Management Association, Chicago, annually.

Press, Charles: *Main Street Politics,* Institute for Community Development, Michigan State University, East Lansing, 1962.

Ridley, Clarence E.: *The Role of the City Manager in Policy Formulation,* International City Management Association, Chicago, 1958.

Schlesinger, Joseph A.: *Ambition and Politics: Political Careers in the United States,* Rand McNally Company, Chicago, 1966.

U.S. Advisory Commission on Intergovernmental Relations: *Urban America and the Federal System,* 1970.

Vidich, A. J., and Joseph Bensman: *Small Town in Mass Society,* Princeton University Press, Princeton, N.J., 1958.

Wahlke, John C., and others: *The Legislative System,* John Wiley & Sons, Inc., New York, 1962.

Wood, Robert C.: *Suburbia—Its People and Their Politics,* Houghton Mifflin Company, Boston, 1959.

INDEX

133